Diary of a Madman

Alucard Esruc

Dedication

This book is dedicated to all my family and friends. This is for the ones that I have lost and the ones still here. Thank you for all the love and the memories. I hope to immortalize you in my works.

Special thanks to Ronald Tompkins for helping put the book together. Some of the poems in this book are also written by him. He told me not to say which ones he wrote but part of this book is also his thank you for all your help.

Table of Contents

Preface

This book was developed to help people cope with everyday life. There is more on a person's mind that anyone can imagine. Our everyday fast paced lives have put us on edge. This book was made to make sure you don't fall off that edge. It's easier to cope when you have hope. It's easier to deal with pain when you know someone is going through the same. I share with you my love, joy, pain, anger and anything else that comes to mind.

Introduction

Diary

Listen
Understand the words from this man
The words I write
Always plays out
With every word I write
Listen to hear what I hear
Read you might see what I see
Think you can feel
What it is like to be me
All my pain and tears
Are all written here
All my love and happiness
The fun even the guns
Lies inside on every line
All the memories past
For this book will forever last
All the heart breaks
In this book forever lay
My endless love
My tattoo tears
My life
All those years
Composed
For this record keeper
It never sleeps
Just waiting for me
To return again
To see what was the outcome of this day
Ready to listen no matter what I say
Loving the way

We sit and talk
Even sometimes taking a walk
This book with a soul
My words it will never let go
Thank you dear diary

Witty

Remember you got two ears and one mouth
Means you need to listen more than you speak
I always think on my feet
My mind sharp as a sword
Always ready for war
My war lies in the mind
We clash all the time
Some may call me Albert Einstein
To me all fine
Mr. know it all
I get the last word to end it all
My needle like insight
Smart mouth without a doubt
I quote nothing
I speak the truth
Grab it from the root
Load up my gun and shoot
My mouth I like to run
Like pulling a loaded gun
I love the feeling of my own tongue
I sass till I get the last
Counter every attack
Always ready to verbalize back
I believe in my utter
I'll never quit
So full of it or full of wit

Counting Crows

There the wind begins to blow
Out the window
A line of crows
I begin to count
One by one
More seem to come
As I look
They are watching me
They seem to see right through me
They begin to pose
Such a familiar soul
Eyes sharp as swords
Waiting to go to war
The black feathers
Told about the bad weather
One by one
They start to leave
I did not finish my count
But I seem to know
Still counting crows

A Game of Chess

Two sides collide
One Black and one white
Day and night
No kings
No queens
No knights
Only pawns
The white moves
The black moves
They meet
Now one must choose to move,
Move wrong they lose
The game has more a steak than a pawn
This game will forever go on
An eternal battle
Or eternal warfare
This game has no cares
The viewpoint, points very clear
All the way to the edge
Pushes off to the ledge
This contest with no respect
All just a test
This struggle to clash
All the way to the last
A dispute
Nothing, but the truth
A conflict with no limits
A standing position
Not to let them get him
All combat
Both ready to attack
Go all the way to their death
In this game of chess

Appearance

To appear
To look good
This is a thing that is misunderstood
Pretentious or flashy
So everyone can turn
When they walk pass me
To dress older
Not puerile like a child
Never sleazy
So no one can tease me
It pleases me to say
That I look good today
By the way
Did you see that car
It was clean, smooth and shiny
Parked in a drive way between a fence
Can you say
What a wonderful appearance

Art of War

A painting of a battle
The way they go to war
The pain and the glory
They way the picture told the story
The war cry
The way some die
The way they fought
No another thought
The blood they spill
All on the other side must die
There is never a question why
This conflict leaves all spirits lit
This clash of two sides
A technique, a struggle
A battle of all troubles
The bloodshed, the carnage
Everything a loud bloody red
The skill
Just a thrill
To watched them be killed
Nothing fake all real
Feel the pain
No pain, no gain
Always something there to fight for
The art of war

The Oath

Your word is your bond
The word that bonds
A bloody secret
To carry to your grave
If it leaves your mouth
That is lights out
Keep till your death
Don't ever speak it
Even if it is the last words left
Never tell
On your oath you cannot fell
Your pledge
Speak it, you're dead
A deadly vow
You can never get out
Once you say the word
Forever open up your curse
A swear to always be there
A testimony
That may leave you lonely
A promise you made
You can never escape
So forbidden
You must keep it hidden
A private matter
Information to never to share
Be mysterious
This is a must
A matter so very serious
Isolated and secluded
Never choose to use it
Things you need to know
When you take an oath

Untouchable

I can't be seen
No one can see me
I only stop for my daughter
Only stop for my grandmother
Those two no other
I only can be pictured rolling
They say you can be touched
But I'm touched only from God
The rest don't try
Just too hard
I ball till I fall
When I fall
My two hands
My two feet
Is all I need
I'm bulletproof speak nothing but the truth
Tattooed from face to feet
I walk with a beat
My own theme song plays
You will hear
If beside you I stay
I bring life to a room
Bring the light to the dark
No one but God can put out my spark
The wind follows me
Just to see
And be around me
I don't need no knife
I don't need to fight
I don't need no gun
I run this with my tongue
I draw in heat from the sun
I'm the rock
I'm the strength for the strong

I'm who they go too
When they feel weak
I pick them up on their feet
I'm a outlaw only follow my God
And its till I fall
Till finally he will end it all
Reach out your hand
Go straight through like a ghost
I'm untouchable

Turn My Sorrow

A empty bottle
With no thoughts of tomorrow
My first memory is the day my mother left me
The eyes of a person who had died
For fourteen years I never once cried
That day my own tears died
Never once even asking why
A two year old full of pride
My heart filled with anger
For the lost of a stranger
From that moment on my heart was in danger
Years of questions
Never learning any lessons
Never counting any of my blessings
I had o die
To finally cry
Not only did I drown in water
I drowned in misery
Thinking that not one would miss me
I woke up to hugs
The first time I felt the love
I now understood tomorrow
The day I turned my sorrow

Time on My Side

Time
It never waits
So you should never wait
But always on your side
You must figure out the time
Never still
It moves
So you must move
It ticks
You tick
So you must be quick
You must keep a steady tick
Keep a steady pace
Time is no race
All the days there
Have been or ever will be with me
The future the present the past
All those times will last
Never go against time
Keep pace and you will be fine
No one can tell you your time
One day you will find
That time was on your side

Time Taker

In the sky
A number drops into time
A time for someone to die
A trip to meet their maker
Everyday a number is called to the taker
So everyday someone has to die
There in the shadow of death
Now you will finally rest
If you past the test
There sitting in at the table
In the presence of our enemies
People that never been a friend to me
There a drink of wine
Then everything will be fine
There you finally catch up with time
Truly meet up with the maker
There in the presence of the
Time taker

Time of Peace

A time to unwind
A time to think
Does this feel like peace?
Can I step outside?
And never think I can die
Is this a dream?
That can never be
Finally no more
Demons inside of me
This could never happen
On this earth
A place where pain can never hurt
This was heaven I thought at first
Can I find this?
Before I rest in peace
This is something I can't have till,
Till I rest in peace
When I rest I hope it is in peace
Let the war leave
I just want a moment of peace

Time Waits for no Man

Don't put off something you can do today
You pushed it to the side
All those yesterdays
Life is full of things we can't explain
Here today gone tomorrow
Quickly life empty like a liquor bottle
So many days
So many things we forget to say
Like the words stay
Like the words love
So many risks not being taken
All to afraid just to find the way
Can't even mustard the strength
So many days we let slip away
I pray for all that read these words
That they are truly heard
Don't let life pass you by
People you love gone in the blink of a eye
Please don't miss out on your fate
Remember time never waits

Regrets

Feeling sorry
Mourn what was it all for
This sense of loss
That can never be tossed
A wish to go back in time
Just a moment to rewind
A flashback, a dream
A nightmare with screams
This thing in the past
Will forever haunt
Something I cannot change
How I wish I died that day
This feeling can never go away
The past I can never change
Why did I do that, that day?
I never can forget
Like the day my heart went away
This feeling of pure pain
Knowing it can happen again
The choices that I make now
In the future
May keep my head down
I must be smart
So I won't have this feeling in my heart
Is this but a test?
Most of my life I seem to regret

Phoenix

I rise and I rise and I rise
I cried when the old me died
But I rise with great fire
When I buried my liar
My eyes are haunted
A cold stare
So much determination so beware
This is not the old me
Be careful I set him free
I'm reborn this passion is everlasting
My rebirth to the world I'm a curse
The new me longs to be free
Dark in a distant
My eyes you can see
The flame of our father
Touches inside my cornea
The fallen angel is no longer fallen
Poems are no longer untitled
I'm a quote from the bible
I'll rise and I'll rise and I'll rise
Never be or finish
An eternal phoenix

Paintbrush

Two eyes look out a window
The eyes are met with color
Inside the eye
A blue sunrise
Beautiful, a sight to see
Bright colorful as can be
Suddenly the colors change
There was a hand
A paintbrush
The greatest artist
To ever pick up a brush
How does he think of this?
Every time I see
It seems to be the most beautiful
Never can wait to see
What new colors will be given to me
New patterns
Some closer some scattered
Some skinny others fatter
Just a delight to pass the night
To wake up again
So the colors and my eyes can meet again
So beautiful, so amazing
Often finding myself starring
The paper that he draws on
Seems to get lost with every stroke
The colors just give me hope
Every time I see
I know I can cope
From dusk to dawn
Such a wondrous paintbrush

Lust for Life

Call me a sinner
For life I will be a winner
My request
Is to live life till my death
Till there is nothing left of me
Giving up and dying something I cannot see
Call it greed
Just something I need
This passion
For my life forever lasting
An appetite to get pass the night
A desire
In my eyes all fire
The anticipation of a new day
Touches my heart in a wonderful way
The eagerness I get
Every time I think about it
The excitement
For every moment I try to savor
Such a wonderful flavor
All intensity inside me
Just an urge that I need to see
A thirst
Thinking about death seems to hurt
I crave for another day
A wish along
Will my life forever go on?
I yearn just to feel the storm
An obsession
Life has taught me so many lessons
I just love the way it keeps me guessing
I relish
Hoping I can never parish
This hunger inside that I must eat

Enjoy just standing on my own feet
I ache for
Like a person's life is at stake
An inspiration knowing a new day is what I'm facing
Call me arrogant
My life no one can prevent
A gift that was truly heaven sent
To live long I repent
Call me selfish
For my life I'm helpless
A glorious feeling
Knowing God is doing the dealing
Seems like I'm always willing
So enthusiastic
Knowing yesterday I got past it
My ambition my happiness
Because life is given
I long just to go on
I'm inspired by the light
Knowing I survive through this night
So magnificent and splendid
That I was chosen to have this
A yearning a longing
Leaves me singing
Call me self-centered
I told you for life I'll be a sinner
This is must
For life I will lust

Ghetto Blues

My life of madness
This place so full of sadness
A place of hell
With a few moments of heaven
This place so full of sin
Seeming that it can never end
A place of war
What is all the fighting for?
So many gun shots
This place is left hot
A modern day Babylon
One day will burn
We are all lost in the storm
Will I be the last one left?
A place of sorrow
Where no one looks for tomorrow
A place so dark that then sun never shines
Without light
How could you find
A place of evil
Things that happen here
Are unbelievable
The feeling that is given
To survive you must start of the killing
This place like a trap
There is no turning back
A living I didn't have the chance to choose
Caught up in the
Ghetto blues

Bulletproof

Everyday I trick my mind
Give myself a motivated speech
Standing in water neck deep
No time for sleep
Sleep is for the weak
Nothing I do is right
Everything is all wrong
But still I press on
Motivate my wrongs
Tricking myself they are right
Trying to ball before I put in the work
Just get my feelings hurt
My life just gets worst
Maybe one day I will see the truth
Till then live like I'm bulletproof

Lost Souls

A valley of spirits
All lost none found
Never knowing the day
Seeming can never find their way
The time
Never on the mind
Never even trying to find
Lost, but never hide
Always easy to find
These hopeless souls
Never worrying about tomorrow
Hearts full of sorrow
Just empty and hollow
Nothing or no one to follow
Head forever down
Just a eternal rain cloud
Never crack a smile
Never wanting anyone around
Tears never run down
Never a care
Just don't want to be here
Just misguided and roaming
Just never knowing
Where they might end up going
Life for these just a dream
There waiting to escape
Not loving this place
To them just a space
Not a resting place
Just lost waiting for their fate
Which always happen too late
For that day they just sit and wait
No plans, no dreams
To them life ain't always what it seems

Life for them cold
The feeling of a Lost soul

A Flush of Shadows

In the night
Darkness overwhelms
Inside lies things that do not tell
Demons and evil spirits
Step inside and hear it
Some fear it
And most always feel it
A mysterious place
Things with an empty face
A space of trapped figures
When the sun comes
No longer by your side
They seem to run and hide
A place only a few have seen
Time never passes
The world could die
But they will always last
It's a battle
To be a part
Of the flush of shadows

Shadow

My mirror image
The sun gives this
All it really needs is some light
With a touch of night
Some may say,
The shadow is my soul
It follows everywhere I go
When I repent
It repents
One day I even seen a shadow of my tear
As it fell from here
Something I can never shake
Or even forsake
I will miss when it's gone
Been with me for so long
Since I was born
It moves as I move
A step, it never lose
I'm never alone
Walks with me home
It gives off the way
I will go that day
My partner in crime
Together we do time
My closet road dog
Still there when I'm wrong
It's my prisoner
And I am the war
Never ask what I am fighting for
When I disagree
He disagree
So someone is always with me
It's never two against one
Together we run

Find us together in the sun
No one, but I know
My shadow

Shortest Way to Hades

Where would you like to be
What is the place you would like to see
The fastest way to get there
Stand in front of
A broken love
To empty the veins of blood
To sell your soul
The devil will never let it go
To curse God to hurt and angel
To be damned
Find yourself in his land
To not believe
Find yourself cursed
When you finally leave this earth
To be evil and murderous
Thus a flush of sins
To except the twisted cross
The love you must toss
Cross good with evil
To commit suicide
To commit a homicide
An never care who dies
To murder in cold blood
To never let a single tear flood
To be full of fire
Just an evil desire
To just hate thee
Find the shortest way to Hades

Sleep to Dream

I don't like to open my eyes
Don't like what I find
I love to dream
Nothing is what it seems
This turns to that
That turns to this
Here I have a child
Oh, how she makes me smile
I have a wife
Together throughout life
All my friends no longer alive
In this world they survive
When I wake
I feel the need to cry
Why did I have to open my eyes
Here my friends
Are there to the end
My family stay beside
Here we can never die
Money doesn't mean a thing in my world
See all my lost loves
Give them all a hug
Life here is sweet
Walking everywhere with just my feet
Sometimes they turn to nightmares
I don't care
Help conquer my fears
I love these things
Sleep to dream

Sands of Time

A desert
Full of empty space
A place all room, no things
Not a soul in sight
It gets cold at night
A place dead as a graveyard
You can move,
But you won't get far
So much space
You will go crazy in this place
No water to taste
Illusions full of confusion
A wasteland
That respects no man
Like the flush of shadows
A battle to live
The sands take and never give
In this place only a few can live
Winds begin and never end
Storms blind
Blow sand into the eye
So much that it burns and you cry
A place of loneliness
That mistake you will regret
It seems this is your death
Try to survive till your last
Were the present meets up with your past
At last you realize you're trapped
With no turning back
The destruction for your mind
Trapped in the sands of time

Sad Eyes Follow

I seem to bring nothing but sorrow
No one knows the troubles I see
But the ones that follow
For me
Praying for a new tomorrow
They seen all my struggles
And counted my many troubles
I hear their sad song
In my head
Forever playing on
"God give shelter to this trouble soul"
"Help him find his way home"
I hear that all day long
If I sit too long
Visions from my past will haunt
Memories I do not want
In the distance
I can see and hear
All the things I came to fear
Flowers dropping to the ground
Hearing the words
Now lay me down
Drown my pain into an empty bottle
Wings and sad eyes follow

One Rainy Day

A window looks outside
See a drop of water
It falls down the glass
It was cold at first
Then it began to warm
It is filled with pain and sorrow
But why because it falls to the ground and die
Or because it seen so much
That it had enough
Through lifetime after lifetime
Spent most of its day crying
Trying not to
Trying not to cry
You can't stop the water from falling
So don't try
To stop the water if you can
That force you can lift a mountain with one hand
So you wonder what's the rain and the window
A tear running down a face of a grown man
One rainy day

Nothing

Nothing matters
Whatever happens let it happen
I have nothing
I am nothing
Nothing at all
Nothing but flesh
Nothing but a heart
That always gets broke
So I gave it away
Nothing but a brain
That voices of the past dead drives me insane
Nothing but a soul
That is lost trying to find its way
Nothing but a soul
Which I can't seem to control
Nothing but a soul
Looking back often wondering did it even get sold
Nothing matters
Nothing

Play My Hand

In my hands I hold four kings
One of hearts
One of diamonds
One of clubs
One of spades
Which one is the first to be played
I can show my hand
but you will never understand the faces of this man
On a different day a different card will be played
With different people this suit
Will find a different bullet to shoot
I play the diamonds a lot
This card can always find the spot
I rarely play the club
I hold this card close
When it causes problems
Were my trump card will have to solve them
I play the spades the most
It's my trump card
It the one that hides the heart
The card that is rarely played
Sometimes it is never seen
I play this hand so well
I always win within three
The forth is never a need
If I ever play that card I will lose
The other will win
My cards not ready to go all in
The many faces of a man
Learning to play his hand

A Heart for the Taking

A man sits and waits
A woman passes by
Catches the eye
Watching her like a hawk
Feels the need to stalk
His feet get up and walk
There his mouth starts to talk
Beautiful what's your name?
Love she said
Love, well I love that name
Thank you
May I take this walk with you?
Yes please by all means
Do you come here a lot?
No, I just came here to find,
To find what?
You, (a smile)
Why me?
It's what my heart told me
What did your heart say?
Sit here and your love will walk this way
Your heart said all that
Yes, it said I will love her to death
So what do you feel?
That this is really real
So you say you love me?
Yes, I have this feeling in my chest,
But you don't know me
So I just listen to what my heart told me
So what now?
I just don't know,
But I'm happy I found
I do seem to love you
Then it is true

Just say I do
I guess I do
I guess the reason I was waiting
Because I had a heart for the taking

Forever Young

In a church
A child sleeps
Not a breath or a peek
Now can never speak
Just a time of peace
Eternal harmony
Nothing can harm thee
Now so free
Just let him be
Calm as ever
No more bad weather
His harmony light as a feather
His youthfulness forever measured
His fresh face
Can put a smile on your face
This everlasting look
Unendingly stay forever with me
His constant look
In my mind never shook
The light on his face
Can never age his face
For me will never be misplaced
He can never grow old
The last story told
There the look on his face so cold
Always and forever
This moment of you
Your face such a young age
In this day
There forever he will lay
There lies the forever young

Eternal Lovers

So many lifelines
Always seeming to be mine
This story forever told
A tail old as the beginning of time
A love that will be forever mine
My beloved dearly
Always yours sincerely
A person always in my heart
Seeming to never be apart
I guess she was always there from the start
This feeling so clear
I guess will always live here
This unconditional love
Travel forever through time
Like the forever rose bud
Everlasting
Time never passing
Two hearts that beat as one
Two songs forever sung
Two souls becoming whole
Grow together and die old
Two pairs of eyes with one view
The vision so great and true
Two bloodlines mixed together
To always escape the bad weather
Two birds of the same feather
Here, now, always forever
Life long memories
Never had a chance to be enemies
These two hearts so deep
The beautiful music can put you to sleep
It could only be covered
With eternal lovers

Hope in the Clouds

I always keep my head up
Walk with my head held high
Straight looking towards the sky
I know the suns there
I can feel the heat
From my head to my feet
I see the stars
Wondering how far
Watching the moon glow
It makes shadows
The reflection of the soul
I believe heaven lies behind the sun
So I stare without a care
Till I see spots in my eye
One day I'll go blind
Staring days at a time
Knowing it's worth it
Just to have one glance
Just a second is worth my sight
Imagine the hope it will bring
How many songs I will sing
I maybe blind but that picture
Will stay in my mind
Burned inside my eye
So when you see this blind man
You see heaven in his eyes
I never keep my head down
Blind and proud
After I see the hope in the clouds

Happy Ending

Finally a peace in my tale
Can't wait to see
What will really happen to me
A joyful finish
A last wish
Again a perfect gift
A satisfying dream
A great final fantasy
Lucky I say
For me to end this way
Complete
This time no defeat
A closing remark
Makes me cheerful in the heart
Fortunate I say
To end this way
Feeling of a crown
Now lay me down
The best conclusion to my question
Jolly and lively
I hope this will be timely
This thrill
I just want to feel
Will it be great as the beginning
My happy ending

Love Doesn't Matter

Be careful
Open your eyes
You will be surprise
They might love you
But they can leave with ease
Never to look back
To see if you will react
They never care
Even if you show a tear
The heart has love
But doesn't care for the love
If you choose to leave
They still stay in one piece
These people pray
That they stay away
If you shall find
Your heart will break in due time
When you find
I hope and pray
That you will leave them behind
If love doesn't matter to a person
You can never hurt them
Feel forsaken
From the heart that was taken
Wishing this is but a dream
Love and hate do not make a good team
That starts off the killing
No reason for living
You will shatter
If you find the person
That love doesn't matter

Love Leaves

Love vanishes
Like smoke in the air
Like a smile on your face
It leaves
Just to torture me
Feels like it ain't for me
Looks straight
And never turn back
Loveless like black and white
Turns from day to night
From love to hate
It never waits
It never hesitates
Like all the tears that ran down your face
It once again leaves this place
Like the air we breathe
It hurts when it leaves
Some leave
Others have no choice
Like you have lost your voice
So many reasons
Like a person laying on the ground bleeding
So many have seen it
They all are thieves
When love chooses to leave

Help Me Believe

My grace a thousand miles away
Started to count the days
Getting harder and harder to pray
My faith seems to come and go only God knows my soul
Watching time pass through an hourglass
The faith instill within me
Will not last
Don't ask me about my past
Because it was all bad
Missing out on a lot of things
I should have had or hadn't
Tend to make me sad
But it hardens the heart
I am falling apart
A suicide haunts the mind
Whispering demons screaming do it
I won't be missed
I just want to quit
And just get rid of this
I'm tired of trying
Everyone else but me is dying
I am losing my will
It's no longer my way
Someone, somewhere give me a reason
Nothing no more has meaning
I just stop believing
I'm lost at being lost
I no longer have a cause
This poem I will leave
Someone help me believe

Always in My Heart

Always a part of me
In my eye your all I see
Where would I be
If I didn't have you by my side
I think I would have died
All the times I cried
There you are to dry my eyes
When I felt pain
You ask to feel
There always there trying to heal
When I'm feeling down
There you are, coming around
When I wanted to fight
There with your hands down
Asking me choose what's right
When I tried to push you away
You was there the next day
When I tried to run
You always seem to find
There is just no place to hide
There in my moment of evil
You brought a cross
I guess that I needed to toss
There trapped in the darkness
You came with the light
Always seeming to set things right
In my moment of loss
You cried with me
Telling that's the way it has to be
When I lost my mind
There you helped me find
When I went crazy
There just to show me that you care
When I lost my blood

Gave me an bandage to stop the flood
When I didn't feel the love
You was there to give me a hug
When I have visions
You ask to see with me
When I traveled through the shadow of death
You was there holding my hand
Telling there no reason to fear this land
When I was there you help me prevail
To make sure I didn't fell
In the time I lost it
There just to comfort
It was all I need to proceed
In the moment I didn't want to breathe
You didn't let the air leave
In my time I want to die
You was there starting to cry
Because of the tear
I guess I do have a reason to stay here
To God, my family and friends
This love is till the end
I guess we can never be a part
For everything you did
You will always be in my heart

For Your Love

What I wouldn't do
To be in love with you
A sucker for this feeling
Always smile when I see
Saying one day it could be me
All the troubles I go through
Just to have you
All the time spent
Trying to have it
All the places I go and been
Hoping one day I will see you again
Journey inside my mind
There it will last a lifetime
A delight knowing this might take a fight
Nothing you do is wrong
Everything is right
Do whatever you can
To hold this in your hand
Make sure that you keep it
Like your bloody secret
A smile on my face
For the moment I can't wait
A wish on a star
Knowing if it leaves it won't be far
Try and try
Never give up
This has nothing to do with luck
This is always in my heart
Sometimes may be a part
Flying free through my heart
Like a dove
What I wouldn't do for your love

My Endless Love

Five years ago
Two high eyes
Past a gift by
The eyes lit up
At this beauty
My eyes felt the need to have
The first time around it didn't last
My eyes and my heart
Starts to talk
The heart told the eyes
Why, why did you make us cry?
I am sorry it was love at first sight
And anyway you didn't put up a fight
So what?
Can't you see no one can love you or me?
Why such harsh things you say?
Remember our own mother went away
That is true
So what now is there left to do?
I guess to be friends
Yes that's a good way to end
But, the heart didn't see it that way
So it chose not to stay away
The eyes understood this
Now that it got back their gift
A year went by
Not a tear fell from the eye
Then the music stopped
Once again my heart dropped
The eyes to the heart
Why must we always fall apart?
It was written
Remembering what happen at the beginning
Another year went by

The heart and the eyes asked why
I guess it wasn't meant to be
No one can love you or me
But still in love
My heart chose to see
I will find a way for the gift to love me
Once again got back the gift
How many times must we deal with this?
But still all happiness and love
Tell once again lost this friend
Heart to the eyes
Shut up and let me cry
What did we do wrong?
I don't know
I guess we just have a sad song
But still the eyes and the heart feels
So once again
They let the gift back in
This time it was different
I guess they really meant it
Happiness again but once again
It started to end
The gift stopped telling the eyes and heart
That they were loved
No longer gave a hug
Never wanted them around
Once again tears started to run down
But this time it was different
The heart and eyes left on their own
Because of the love that wasn't received
Eyes and heart
Why doesn't anyone love you or me?
That it is us that they need
Just someone come hug me
A year past
Dare my heart ask?

Where is the gift
Once again you ask this again
Have you not cried enough?
It made us cry more than anything dead or alive
Aren't you tired of being hurt?
Yes but it was worth what it was worth
True so once again
The gift came back into my life again
This time the heart and the eyes
Gave the gift pain
And said it would never happen again
If the heart and eyes feels loved too late
I see that they will run and escape
I guess all the eyes and heart
Really needed
Was the feeling of love and being needed
Since the gift showed back in the day
I guess the eyes and heart can't stay away
But the gift isn't very affectionate
So they both guessed it
Let it fly
Like it let us fly
Maybe it will come back to you
Like the way you came back it
The eyes and heart are once again
Filled with pain
Knowing they may never see
Their endless love again

Love

Do you love me?
Because I love you
Tell me that you love me?
I need you
Do you need me?
Please do tell me
You're my beloved?
Am I your beloved?
Please tell me
You're my sweetheart
Do I have your heart?
I adore you
Do you adore me?
I cherish you
Do you cherish me?
Am I all you see?
I appreciate everything you do
Tell me you feel the same way too
I want to spend the rest of my life with you
I hope it is me you choose
I can't lose you
Can you lose me?
Dare I say?
My life I can have it no other way
Tell me that you will stay
Come share my world
Can I share yours?
Take my hand
Can I take yours?
You're what I am living for
Am I what you are living for?
Just say it is all you can see
Why won't you tell me you love me

Mad Love

Crazy
So crazy
The way I feel
No one
I mean no one can stop me from having it
No can stand in my way
I will cause you pain that day
I don't mean to be mean,
But this feeling is all I seen
This feeling so strong
I don't even care if it is wrong
All right in my eye sight
A sweet, sweet desire
In my soul all fire
I'm a mad man for this love
Crazy
Just stay away from me
A lunatic
Without it I am sick
A psycho
Can never let go
It can never leave
You minus well just kill me
It can never go free
Unless beside me
This look in my eye
For this I will gladly die
This uncontrollable pulse
I will haunt as a ghost
I seem to need this the most
It cannot be removed
Once I choose
There is nothing you can do
I won't stop till I have you

I'm a person that you can never shake
Believe me I will do whatever it takes
Don't tell me I'm too late
This will be our fate
An emotion that can never wait
No one can ever forsake
I will gladly
Love you madly

What You Do to Me

Oh you don't know
what you do to me
so let me tell you
These words are true
I share things that never should be told
always saying I'm old
With me you always have a home
No need to have a night alone
With you I share my bed
Make it comfortable
so beautiful dreams can dance in your head
I kiss you on your cheeks at night
A lovely view
To wake and see you in my sight
I hold you in my arms
To make you feel safe and warm
With you I show my affectionate side
The part of me I hide
Not many know my soul
I hope my strength
Follow you where ever you go
I long to kiss her neck
I'm an jerk but show her nothing but respect
I know I come on strong
I'm sorry I'm nothing but strong
I give her my all
Cause that's all I can give
the only way I know how to live
I often find my hands on her body
I let her curves guide me
I shall immortalize you in my words
Immortality shall keep in this book
my brown sugar so soft so sweet
All of our secrets I will keep

Even though she may never see
What she does to me

Use Your Heart

Close your eyes
Use your heart to see
The eyes are often blind
So use your heart to find
It sees and knows things
Your eyes can't pick up
Let your heart roam free
Now open your eyes you can see
Feel the magic
Listen to your heart
So you will not be far apart
There all your answers lie in your heart
No more questions
You have learned all your lessons
It tells no lie
Open like the eye
Go deep inside
The truth you will find
Don't be afraid to listen to the voice
Once your heart is open
You have but one choice
Let the voice tattoo inside you
Then you will see
Now your heart is free
Have the courage to follow
So you and your heart will awake tomorrow
Never be afraid to shed a tear
Your heart will help you lose that fear
Never be afraid to ask your heart questions
Without it you won't learn any lessons
Always keep it pure and true
So you will always know what to do
Listen to these words and be smart
Remember to always use your heart

Too Late For Tears

A regret
That I will have to the death
A reason why,
Why now should I cry
It kind of late
Now its left to fate
This feeling I can't escape
I just should have wait
I should have thought
I never seem to think
I just do
Just the choices I choose
Will I win or lose
This feeling of unforgiving
I stopped a person from living
I took away everything he had
Now just a memory of the past
How long will this feeling last
How could I
Now I feel the need to cry
I wish I could change time
Rewind so all would be fine
I thought it would be easy the first time
I see I was wrong
This feeling seems to go on and on
Like I'm lost in the storm
Now I write this poem
Days and years pass,
But still it haunts
Sometimes I wish it would stop
Always feeling like a tear will drop
What will stop this pain
To take another person's life again
I guess that will just cause more pain

Yet still driving me insane
It always stays on my brain
Time and time again
Is this fear, should I cry
Or is it too late for tears

The Craze

There one day
One man start to say
Did you hear that sound?
Like a pain to the ear
What the sound of a tear
Someone cries, but from whom
Everyone else has died
Then the sound rose
And flared up his nose
Who goes?
Who goes there not a word to comfort the ear
The heart race fast in a pace
It beats loud makes the blood run wild
Am I going crazy or just losing my mind
No ticking from time
A slow motion lunatic potion
Everything stuck just my luck
Can't move stiff trying to get a grip
Then a tick I regain
Time move once again
What happen to this pain?
It felt like the breaking of a heart
Till death did them part
Am I going mad?
What was that?
Finally I got my senses back
Then in a flash
A cold death chill passed
Who goes who goes?
An angel to take to hell
But why
You know what you did
Why me you come and seek
I was told to come get your soul

Its mine come, back another time
You can run but not hide
There is no turning back
You will regret where you end up after death
I am sorry for that tear
For you to lose that fear
Take my hand
Follow me to my land
No, no I will not go
You have no choice
Don't cry, dry your eyes
A blink closed eyes
A crash
It was all a dream
Open his eyes heard eternal screams

The Cold

The comfort of the wind
Can't wait till Winter begin
A tear for Winter's end
A delight
It gets colder at night
Outside
Standing in cold proud
The wind blows load and fierce
The cold seems to pierce
The cold storm
So how it keeps me warn
I seems as if I was born
To get lost In a storm
The snow and ice
Makes my eyes glow at night
The cold wind
Seems to be my friend
Always at peace
When I go to sleep
All the secrets that lies in the snow
Seems to silence my soul
I guess this is so
I was born in a storm
My love seems to grow
When I'm trapped in the cold

Suicide

Should I live?
Should I die?
Someone, give me a reason why,
Why am I living?
Why do I breathe?
Why should I see?
Why should I even think?
I should blow out my brains
Or just empty a vein
I don't want to live this life again
Just the thought of me living
Makes me want to start off my killing
I don't want to live
I don't want to see
To wake up again
Just one more moment of pain
I think will drive me insane
A thought of a new tomorrow
Seems to leave me hollow
I'll send myself to hell
I don't care if I fell
This feeling so strong
I don't know how long I can go on
Someone please put me out of my misery
Somebody make me history
All the death and lies
I don't ever want to cry
Now it's my time to die
No more living
No more people giving
No more wishing
No more dreaming
No more love
No more hate

No more seeing this face
No more pain
No more demons
No more voices
No more left with choices
No more wrongs
No more rights
No more lonely nights
Time never on my side
It's time to do my suicide

Eternally Bleeding

Most people blood flows
Me I bleed on the inside
Sometimes I wish I just die
Forever crying on the inside
My soul isn't in my control
My heart beats and stops
When it feels
My heart breaks
From time to time
It always seems to die
My eyes are wide shut
Open but blind
My feelings are mixed
Because of all this
The pain inside my brain
Trapped making me insane
The things I have seen
Makes my eyes bleed
The cuts and wounds the scares
All of my war marks
My tattoo tears
For my life in all those years
A thug pumping slugs
An outlaw till I fall
I only follow my God
My life so very hard
Things seems to catch me off guard
Am I cursed
My prison is the earth
Seems never believing
Forever eternally bleeding

Death of Love

To lose a love
Is to lose a heart
To lose a heart
Is to fall apart
To lose a connection
Is to lose apart of you
A connection hoping forever a resurrection
When it dies it leaves in sections
The eyes are often blind
You see things but cannot find
The heart breaks
In no time it takes
The soul depletes
Tears start to leak
The ears close
You cannot hear
Even if their standing right there
The body dies
Because of all tears you cried
It will take time
Again to make these things mine
This parting of hearts
This true feeling of loss
Which I came across
I feel deceased
Even though my heart is free
What is to become of me
This demise
Made my heart die
What is left
It was love
Now it is death

Blind Men See

In a distance
A figure with sunglasses
I often wonder about the sunglasses
A walking stick as he passes
He begin to smile
It stayed there for a while
It is like he seen me
Like his eyes was free
I stopped
He stopped and turned
I bet that keeps you warm
What do you mean?
The sweater maybe green
Why do you have a stick if you can see?
For reasons of people like me
But how did you know
Think about it
It is cold
Oh yes so you guessed
If you want to say that
By the way nice hat
What how could this be
Do blind men really see

Strange Vision

Two burry eyes see
Something different from you or me
The eyes look out
As if it was a gift to see
Even though their vision is burry
The eyes stare as a pair
Looking as if someone was there
It was bizarre
Because I seen no one near or far
It was odd
There he begin to talk
Then I stared again
No one even in a distant
He must have had a very unusual view
I stared deep
Almost putting myself to sleep
But still no one was there
Thinking why did I even care
I stayed and looked
All the time it took
He stayed talking
Still I see no one walking
His vision must be diverse
At least that is what I thought
His unique unlike insight
Separate from my eyesight
Smeared through the night
It was very peculiar to me
Still I couldn't see
I guess this vision varies from me
But why I have wonderful sight to see
It was weird
I still hear him speak
What is it that he sees?

Like it was blotch from me
I walk up to him
Please tell me what you see
He said your sight is distinctive from me
What do you mean?
It was only to find
That I was blind

The Eyes

These eyes my eyes
Look into my eyes
Tell me what you see
Do you see the hate?
Do you see the past memories?
The flashbacks of the bad times
With little memory of the good times
My eyes filled with demons and evil spirits
My eyes of pain
Don't stare too long
Or you will never be the same
My eyes the search for love
But never seem to find
But when my eyes find
It always leaves
My eyes full of hopes and dreams
They can see them
But they are so far very far away
My eyes that need love in order to survive
My eyes that Lord only knows how I tried
My eyes quiet but bold
You look to deep my life story will unfold
My eyes seen things that others can't imagine
My eyes say that you should never want to see
My eyes cry because of my past memories
My eyes search for someone to touch and hold them
But no one's ever around when my tears start to run down
My eyes of darkness searching for the light
For that sunshine to make them stop crying
The eyes my eyes
The evil snake eyes
The windows to my soul

Tattoo Tears

An arm of faith
For the one who has create
A chest of good and evil
For both sides of the sky
The things that drives you and I
A chest of pleasure and pain
Two feelings you will feel again and again
A leg of a warrior
For the spirit inside that drives
A stomach of an outlaw
Because I only follow my God
It's till I fall
A neck of a dragon
For the power that lies deep inside
A back of death
Because I am the last one left
An arm of a snake
For the time I spent doing his ways
A finger of a gangster
For all the guns I held in my hand
A finger from DC
It will always be a part of me
An arm of a lost soul
For the time I couldn't control my mind
An arm of a sword
For all the times I went to war
An arm for a sucker
Because that's how I am for love
A hand of a rose
For the life I chose
An arm of darkness and light
A person of darkness
In search of his light
Which could only be love

A finger of loneliness
I guess I will be to my death
A hand of a heart and a sword
The reasons I live for
An eye of a cross
Because now I'm in the eye of God
My life in all those years
My tattoo tears

Study of Shadows

Night is when I creep
To find the things that does not sleep
I stand silent believe what I am seeing
Keeping a slow steady breathing
Hearing footsteps but no ones left
Hearing voices but no one's there
This old castle full of bones
A place for the dead to find a home
The world full of the treasure
They can't leave behind
So they stick around
To once again they are found
I hide in places
To try to recognize the faces
So hard to be in the right place
Things move and fall
With no touch at all
God bless for one day
May they rest
Every day I pay them respect
This life that they never left
True secrets will be kept
Their starting to be like a buddy
These shadows I study

Death Before Dying

A man lays
Watching the clock
Every tick, every tock
Every second
Like waiting for the reckoning
Nothing moves but his eyes
Following the clock
Lock like a safe
Waiting for something to happen
Waiting for the right time
To move more than his eyes
Time waits for no man
No movement
Thinking he will lose it
The back ground black
Nothing but a clock
The sounds tick tock
As if he knew it would stop
Focus seeming so hopeless
Stuck never giving up
Just his luck it stopped
A very loud tock
No more movement from the clock
No more movement from the eye
The clock had died

Demons Surround Me

My surroundings
My world
They follow
Hoping, praying that they don't return tomorrow
These fast moving free spirits
Seems only I can hear it
Twilight of the day, twilight of the night
Just a fight
To find what's wrong, what's right
No one there to help
No one ever seems to see but me
Are they mines to hold
Seeming to bother me the most
These evil creatures
With hellish features
They lurk I feel I am cursed
Trapped with no turning back
If I look back
They are ready to attack
I try to run and never come back
But still there
When I finally reach here
Always by my side
Will they leave if I die
Always laughing
When I cry
If you come around
You shall see
That the demons surrounds me

All That Remains

Two guns stare
Both without a care
Quiet full of desire
They both sit and wait
But still never hesitate
This moment sounds all around
Knowing what's about to go down
Trapped in time
The moment of truth they will find
Two large figures
Lay beside their heads
Both a loud red
The two figures
Leave smile on the trigger
The smoking barrels
No more hello
At the moment they lay
Feels the need to stay
They sit there and rest
Memories of the blood feast
They stay and endure
Their laying on the floor
Both stare at thee
Just seconds they was enemies
This time of grief
For the guns
A time of relief
Finally some peace
From the shells to the soul
A part that they had to let go
No tears
Never had a single fear
What a shame

The way they played that game
Now this is all that remains

Drink Away the Pain

A shaking hand
In his hand a glass
The glass full of thoughts
Memories of how life use to be
This moment seems so hopeless
At the point of strike
Hoping to pass out
And not remember this night
As the glass moves closer to his face
Things start to move in this place
The mind starts to think
All his thoughts start to sink
The thought of this last glass
Will make this feeling pass
Now his voice starts to drag
At last
No more ever having to ask why
Do I even try
Having the feeling to cry
Finally the glass touches the lip
Took it all down not a sip
So he slips away
No more pain of living this day
But I know once again
Another day
He will be here
To drink away the pain

Broken Pieces

Everywhere I look, I see small pieces
All was once a part of my life
Can't seem to get anything right
I use to have so many dreams
But my life never
Turns out the way I wanted it to be
I remember when I was happy
But that faded away
Like it was a part of yesterday
Nothing ever went my way
I found myself lost and confused
Not knowing what do to
I did everything wrong
Couldn't seem to do anything right
It was and still is
Hard to sleep at night
I hear voices in my head
Am I better off dead?
A lot of people tried to help
I should have open up my hand
A lot of people told me what was right
I should have listen
I was so young
What did I know about life?
So many bad memories
Life has never been a friend to me
As the time goes by
A lot of old things I find
I continue to find myself
Along the way I remember this
When I pick up the broken pieces

A Thousand

A thousand drops of blood
A thousand times I loved
A thousand people dead
A thousand tears I shed
A thousand rests in the same bed
A thousand years I been here
For a thousand years I shed tears
A thousand fears
A thousand memories so clear
A thousand lies
A thousand people had to die
Another thousand tears I cry
A thousand wars
Preparing for a thousand more
A thousand breathes
Only a thousand more left
A thousand roads
A thousand ways to go
A thousand uncertainties
A thousand people inside of me
A thousand songs
A thousand still play on
A thousand wrongs
A thousand rights
Only a thousand people
Truly living life
A thousand thoughts
A thousand things fought
A thousand touches of grace
A thousand smiles on a face
A thousand innocent
A thousand ignorant
A thousand things I know
A thousand things I don't know

A thousand roads home
A thousand kings
A thousand rings
A thousand sons of man
A thousand cards
A thousand that believe in God
A thousand children
A thousand not living
A thousand only giving
A thousand crimes
Just a thousand times

Walk a Mile in My Shoes

To take a step
To put on someone shoes other than yours
All aboard
You're in for the ride of your life
You're taking my place
You may not survive through the night
To have someone else pain
To walk miles
To look through someone else eyes
To witness all those you don't know die
To see what that person sees
Sometimes is different from you to me
To understand what makes that person
To feel someone else blood flow
To just feel their pain
After that
Never walk in their shoes again
To feel their heart beat
See what drives them crazy
To witness their love
To go down the road they choose
To feel their soul
To see how they feel about things
To hear their inner demons
In their minds steady screaming
To share their joy
To witness their defeat
To see what they eat
To walk with their feet
Feel their tears leak
To speak their words
To see their secrets
Knowing you better keep it
To feel their lose of blood

To see all the lost loves
All this is true
Walk a mile in my shoes
And you would be crazy too

This Woman's Work

The second creator of life
I know you got life left
Guided me through my steps
The second maker of the world
Always be my main girl
Such a wonderful hand
You lay upon this land
You destroy and create
Bless us and curse us
Many sorrows you brought on this world
Many gifts you gave to this world
You lead us to glory days
You lead us to horror days
So many went a stray
From the ways
When we was taught to play
You share your love
You share your hate
On the ones you help create
Steady trapping us in our fates
Is it a blessing or a curse?
This woman's work

The Perfect Gift

As I look out and see
At this gift God has giving to me
All that it cost
Was a rib to give
The most beautifulness thing
To ever cross my eyesight
Just a blessing for it to stay the night
A diamond that shines
Will do anything to make it mine
A wonderful feeling
From the love that is giving
This special thing
To some you must sing
Others will do anything
A dream that has come true
When I look at this
I don't know what to do
To keep away the pain
To make sure the gift comes back again
To take away the fear
Never make shed a tear
To dress up real fine
Put another diamond on a diamond
To make it all mines
Just to have
I will trap in an hourglass
To protect from the storm
Give my clothes to kept it warm
To give my last dime
To love lifetime after lifetime
Every look to cherish
For this gift I will parish
This gift you can't help but to love
Knowing that it could

Only have come from above
The inside can never be ripped
God sent us the perfect gift

Someone to Love

A wish, a dream
Something that is often never seen
For some they never find
Even before dying
For those who find
Sometimes it takes a lifetime
Have some good times
To all the others just,
Just a fantasy
That wishes could be
True love will never leave
It seem like destiny
This is a thing
That all should have,
But sometimes can never be
Be ready and never let them go
When you find someone to love

Sex

Wonderful as can be
For filling always willing
Always can be good
But often misunderstood
Only great when love touches this place
Even after it last
Forever there when time pass
Without love
It leaves like every time you breathe
Unfulfilled just a thrill
Time passes so fast
After the feeling it never last
Seems like a second
Just a breath of heaven
When it stays
Those are the most wonderful days
Often leaving in a daze
There in a maze
You never want to escape
When love is there it is at its best
This is the greatest sex

Dangerous Beauty

The look of a tiger
A look that looks into your soul
A smile like a sunrise
To just have one more look you can die
The face of an angel
Just to see and not touch
Is just to be
The skin soft as a rose
Just to feel it next to you
You will give a piece of your soul
The hair of silk
Not to touch but to hold
A soul so beautiful and clear
Get close and hear a song to your ear
The soul so warm
It can shelter you from a storm
The body of a goddess
What you would do just to have it next to you
A heart so pure and true
When you feel the love
You don't know what you will do
The mind of a genius
The smarts only a few have seen
The lips soft, so sweet
Like sugar addictive with a touch
An enchanting smell
That will put you in a spell
The warmth that is given
Is this my reason for living?
A touch from the hand
Will make you forget you live in this land
An ear of comfort
To hear every word you speak
Just the feeling that is giving

The most dangerous thing alive
Beauty

All My Love

Swallow I give you more tomorrow
Nothing hurts like the mouth
Nothings brings joy like the mouth
So out my mouth
My love will come out
Ain't no doubt
Or doubting the way I feel
For you I'll keep it real
Even love when you are wrong
I'll tell you you're right
Just to see you smile
Your smile brings light
It gives me life
My love of my life
Your beauty is dangerous to me
I try to always use my heart
Whether you're near or a part
My heart is your home
Home is where the heart is
Or where mine live
With you I never take always give
I feel you were sent from above
Here is all my love

Here is All My Love

I will give every drop
Let it rain like my blood
Until every space it flood
Let it be like the ocean
And give life to all
Let it be like fire
And consume all it touches
Let it be like food
And calm all your hunger
Let it be like the snow
Turns everything cold
Let it be like life
And bring many happy years
Let it be like happiness
And take away all your tears
Let it be like vision
A gift to all that's living
Let it be like a rock
Always there
Taking a beating but still there
Let it shine bright like the sun
My love you are the only one
Let it be like the moon
And bring sight to the night
Let it be like a wolf pack
And watch each other's back
Let it be like a mother
Let it be like Jesus and God
The love just won't be hard
Let it be like my wife
Because of her
Never having a lonely night
Let it just come from above
Here is all my love

Enduring Heaven Myth

Someone explain my tears
How I lost all my fears
You ask and believe
You will receive
Mine came in a dream
I ask to see the myth
I began to walk up some stairs
It was dark not a single fear was in here
A man in a room I will try to describe
A dark room with a window
Bright as can be
Light you can truly see
But the light not even enter the room
That was strange never forget that day
Come he said my son
You ask and you shall receive
All because you truly believe
All of a sudden the room vanished
I seen beauty that I cannot explain or describe
Not even with my best eye
Or with this gift that I write
Not even my wildest dream
Could tell you what I seen
This was my gift
The enduring heaven myth

Hallelujah

I heard there was a word
If said would please the lord
The word is love
Shake the heavens from above
Hallelujah
If was said part the holy dark
Yes dark is holy made by the lord
Hallelujah
I will play this cord
To bring the rain down from the lord
After the rain the sun will shine
Bring new colors to the eye
Hallelujah
I once was loved
Known she stares down from the heavens above
Hallelujah
I often wonder
I often wished
Till this day I cherish that gift
She knows how much she is missed
Hallelujah
I miss her voice
I miss her smile
I miss her kiss
To dream of her is my only wish
Hallelujah
I am sinner
In this life to become a winner
I don't always do what is right
Everyday is a fight
With my last breath
I lust for my life
Hallelujah
I often wonder into a storm

To recall the day I was born
Through this cold I still get warm
Finding pages of the book that is torn
To collect the pages that warn
Sometimes it is cold
Sometimes it is lonely
But still I find
Beautiful memories in my mind
hallelujah
Things can get lost with time
The love I share is nothing but mines
Can't erase it with the sands of time
My heart is full of drive
Nothing but fire in my eyes
The window where the spirit lies
The place to find all the tears I cried
Only the lord knows I tried
At his table when I die
Hallelujah

City of Angels

A city full of spirits
Only a few will feel it
Eyes all around
Nothing lost, everything found
These figures mostly seen by a child
We think they are looking at nothing
When they smile
To protect and never neglect
For this city you must have respect
Free spirits
By your side day and night
To get in your mind
They never have to fight
It is everything that is right
Close your eyes and take flight
Some will appear by the light
This place mysterious and true
They are the reasons
You do some of the things you do
All around whispering voices
That tries to give you choices
Listen and understand
The good that can come from this land
Don't be afraid to take their hand
More helpful than any man
All your questions can be answered
In the city of angels

Eye of God

Two eyes everywhere
Over here, over there
Forever watching
Seeming to know
Every move you do before you choose
These eyes never seem to close
Always quiet but bold
These eternal peepers
Have no time for sleepers
These windows all around
Always watching looking down
The eyes never have to move
So large that they can see right through you
The purest and most beautiful eyes
You will meet face to face when you die
The eyes so loved
The eyes so feared
The longer you share
You will shed a tear
These eyes of mercy and compassion
Knowing it will be forever lasting
These loved eyes
Look to long grantee you will cry
To comfort thy staff, thy rod
When you're in the eyes of God

Heaven on Earth

Heaven on earth
And just what would that be
Let me see
This get deep, deep
So deep that you must climb in with both feet
You asked what is heaven in this hell
Please go on do tell
That heaven is love the only thing that is pure
The only thing that can guide you to the light
And or guide you right
With all this darkness
That is so heartless
Love is so powerful
That it can change the eye of crazed man
Make all your tears dry
With a wipe of a hand
Love is worth what it's worth
Yes you better find if you want
Heaven on earth

Hell on Earth

Hell
What is hell?
Earth I say
We are all lost souls
Some find and some will not
Demons enter minds from time to time
Saying there is no need for crying
Suck it up I don't care
Fill you with hate
There is no escape
Don't believe
Just wait and you will see
The flame trapped in every boy and girl brain
Release their pain on the earth and her children
Destroying lives
Selling souls to get some control
But was is it worth what it's worth
No this is hell on earth

A Place of Shadows

Welcome to my world
Will you enter?
Be warned
An eternal storm
A place of souls
Some lost, some found
He steps in with a grin
Not knowing he can never return
He enters with excitement and delight
No knowing it will forever stay night
Not knowing his fate
He enters the gate
And sealed his fate
He can never return
Never return outside this gate
Never knowing what will wait
What is this place?
Nothing
Just an eternal space or a resting place
Who said that?
Just remember you can never go back
What do you mean?
This is just a dream
And so that is what you think
What do you mean?
It has to be a dream
I feel no pain
Listen to me again
Just eternal space or a resting place

Judgment of a Child

A child plays in the grass
So happy time never pass
The child having fun
Feels the need to run
All of a sudden
Stopped by a large figure
It came closer and closer
Then runs right through the child
Like a ghost on a path
The child never had a chance
The taste of death
Is all that is left
The spirit looks out
Only to find out
That this was a chosen route
Two doors open
Two paths to choose
One you win
The other you lose
One door is done
The other just a place to run
The child sits
And must decide
At this point there is no ticking from time
The fates awaits the choice
I hope he listens to that voice
Since the child knows not what he do
He is left with his own choice to choose
Just pray he chooses wise
The profile of
The judgment of a child

Last Breath

A woman lays in a bed
There resting her head
The time has finally come
For her soul and afterlife to become one
There in the bed
Angels dance over her head
Her memories all happy
Glad to had live
Memories of old, everything she did
A great life she got to live
All the time she chose to give
There as time pass
Knowing she's down to her last
For her no fear
Her new life so clear
Not a single reason to shed a tear
A long life she had
So she cannot ever be sad
She awaits this
Like her first gift
Finally true happiness
A place just to be
All the time roam free
A smile always on the face
Pain not even a trace
There she knows
Old family and friends await
Once again to see her face
A tear falls from the eye
All happiness is why
The time has come nothing left undone
Life for her nothing, but fun
Time to go nothing is left

A moment of silence
For her one last breath

Heart Stops

I place my hand on my chest
To feel it beat
Knowing no day it will cease
For years so strong
Now steady getting weak
Softly it now beats
It use to beat hard
Pump my blood so far
Now it skips
Just to get a grip
Still proud
But now getting closer
To lay me down to rest
Knowing one day
That will be the best
Finally it can rest
Keeps beating till my death
I won't stop till I drop
That day my heart stops

Still I Rise

Life's so hard
Things catch me off guard
I lost so many dogs
Like throwing away pennies
Nobody cares
They didn't even see them there
Ain't no love here
Shed so many tears
I dodge gun shots
I sold rocks
I got held at gun point
The point straight to the brain
Lost in the game
Steady going insane
I smoked weed
Drink Hennessey
Roam the streets
Till it's time to eat
I grow up in the ghetto
I live in the projects
Got lost in the gutter
I played in the hood
Always up to no good
I got chased by cops
On pursuit till I drop
I have been alone
One day outside was my home
I slept outside
There at that moment
I lost all my pride
Roaches and rats all around
Afraid to play on the ground
So many hungry nights
So many times I fight

Never ever loving my life
This can't be right
Often wishing for some light
So many nightmares
Wishing someone cared
I went the wrong way
The cause of all my long days
I followed evil spirits
The devil I followed
Will I even see tomorrow?
Yes, I guess I did
God is the reason I still live
Often trap tears in my eyes
But still I rise

My Own Prison

A curse, a place I cannot escape
Is this my destine place
Small but full of space
A trap
To late can never turn back
A path that is already chose
It is like all is out of my control
Everything seen but I can't touch
I seem to reach out so much
Always reaching out my hand
But moves whenever I do
It plays with my mind
Telling me I am running out of time
Always laughing
While people stay
Watching me snapping
This dungeon of keepsakes
I just sit here and wait
A sanctuary of time
Why does it have to be mine?
My tracks my trails
My own living hell
This passage, this route
My prison without a doubt

My Own Prison Closed Eyes

Every blink I feel trapped
Every closed eye
Feel as if I will die
I can't see
Afraid to sleep
Thinking about the secrets it keeps
Hard for even a tear to leak,
But some how
I know when it's night
I know when it's day
The lids closed so tight
Not a trace of light
Or a trail of sight
No visions
I feel I am not even living
I'm in nothingness
Cannot tell me this is not death
I can't wait to dream
Even though it keeps secrets
It's the only time I get to see
Can't even cry
My prison with closed eyes

No Laughing Matter

Hee hee
What's so funny?
Do you find this amusing?
What are you losing?
Your mind
No it just amuses me so
How is this?
This profile not fit for a child
Hee hee
Stop laughing at me
Why
It is not funny to see a person cry
To you, but to me it's funny
Go away and never come back another day
Just go away
No, I have no reason to leave
You're the person I came to see
What is your reason for seeing me?
I cannot tell
If you can't tell then go
No it's you that they chose
Chose for what
Can't you see I had enough?
Yes, but this is for the best
How is this for my best?
When you laugh when I cry
If you open your mind you will see
This lesson for thee
What lesson for me
What can that possibly be?
This is for your eyes to see
What must I see?
How it is best to be, just look at me
What are you talking about?

It's up to you to figure out
Now it's time for me to go
Why did he leave?
What did he forget to tell me?
Did I need to here laugher
In this no laughing matter

Scattered Dreams

In the background a mirror
Closer and closer
It turns clearer
I feel the need to touch
Here, now and forever
The mirror has broken up
The broken glass
All looks different
When I pass
No longer complete
Now all its own piece
Every fragment
Holds its own theme
All scattered dreams

One Last Dance

Two lovers torn
Lost from the storm
Their wondering eyes
Tells no lies
The eyes look around
Too finally they stop and look each other down
The eyes filled with a sunrise
Both start to cry
They both get closer
Till finally face to face
Caught up in the moment
They can't wait
They start to touch
The bringing of the souls
Make their blood rush
They never speak
Knowing tears will start to leak
They begin to move with the music
So lost they can never lose it
The movement, the motion
So beautiful like the waves of a ocean
A quiet storm starts to form
The silence so golden
Hoping that they
Forever stay in this moment
Feeling like they are floating air
In their minds there is no other care
The memories start to flood
Never forgetting about their lost love
The slow dance
Leaves them both in a trance
Will this truly be?
The last dance

Truth or Dare

Let me see
What will you choose?
To be safe or take a risk
To be safe you must tell the truth
To take a risk you must go all the way
A challenge
Are you willing to take?
You know what is at stake
Try this
I bet you will always remember it
Will you take the chance till your last?
Or will you take to keep it safe
Either way
A lot of things will come out that day
Secrets
In this game you cannot keep it,
But are you willing to tell
The things that are lock in the cell
Beware more at stake then you think
So I think should not blink
Always think before you speak
Things there, will start to leak
Before you play
You should think on it that day
They may make you do things
That you would never do
Make you say things you never want to say
All might go down that day
Think before you choose
You might have to say
Things that you don't want to lose
There is no cares
In this game of truth or dare

Pleasure and Pain

Two things we will forever feel
One feels good
The other feels bad
One can make you happy
The other can make you sad
One aches
The other feels great
The way you choose your life
Will determine what you feel that night
One is love
One is hate
One is evil
One is good
Never get them misunderstood
Pain can be pleasure
Pleasure can be pain
The feelings of the insane
Or the way you intrepid in your brain
Laugher, people crying
People living, some dying
These two feelings
Life forever will be giving
Again and again
On and on
"Quote the raven forever more"
Like day and night
Life and death
Yen and yang
We will forever feel
Pleasure and pain

Never Dreamed

Imagine
A person that never dreams
When they close their eyes nothing seen
All darkness when they sleep
Memories they can never keep
A fantasy that can never be
No illusions, no sight
Seems like forever night
Never a vision
From the life that was given
Never a moment of their life
Everything is on hold
Their life seems so cold
Visions never given
Reserved
Only their curse
Never can visualize
All dead in the eye
Something that can never be prevented
To maintain
A want of a memory in his brain
Never to dream, can drive you insane
It is like a nightmare
To never sleep a single thing
A feeling of deep loneliness
Or a person that has never dreamed

One Way In

A route with one way
There is no way out
Just a straight narrow route
A long path
No lefts, no rights
No light to guide at night
One direction
So direct
No turning back even for death
A choice that can never be chosen again
Sometimes feeling it is the end
A road I have to follow
Never a new choice tomorrow
Look back never
A trial I will continue to move
Never a thought to lose
It can never fade
Last with me all my days
A quest
Nothing less
An approach I will comply with
Obey till my dying day
Never surrender or depart
Strait like the start
Leave, something to never think
I will progress till my death
Till there is not a piece of me left
Pursue is something I will forever do
Strive till I die
Seek till I am deceased
Grasp till my last
Stalk with all my heart
Go on even if there is a storm
I will never disappear

Even if I had it up to here
Never again will I fear
The path I chose so clear
Never deteriorate
Even if all I am left with is hate
Never dissolve or retreat
Get back up
Even when I am knocked off my feet
Never care if I sleep
A move I choose to do
This is my route
One way in no way out

Storm of Dreams

I'm haunted by my past
Inside will forever last
My past seems like my future
I will see it again
Like an old friend
It will be there
Showing me no love or care
Don't nobody knows my troubles with God
Made my life nothing but hard
My yesterday never went away
My tomorrow will be haunted by the forty bottle
Every smell of weed
Reminds me of my evil deeds
When I go to sleep at night
In my dreams
I do nothing but fight
Life is calling me back out to the late night
I lost all my pride
Because of the thorns in my side
Nothing is what it seems
When you have a storm of dreams

Live Above Hell

I never really learned
But I'm still trying
All my life nothing but a hell spawn
Now to heaven I try to press on
I must live above ground
And not below
Must figure out a way
To save my soul
I'm in the eyes of god
Now everything is hard
But then again it is easy
All the rules
I must choose to follow
No longer empty and hollow
All has a meaning
Nothing is without a reason
I can say now I love my life
I care about the wrongs
And I know my rights
My will is well
Trying to live above hell

Broken Wings

I spread my wings
And try to fly
Can't even touch the beginning of the sky
I can look up as far as I want to
But there is nothing I can do
My wings are hurts
From traveling through the earth
I can hear you calling me home
But I can't get there on my own
I am turning more and more human everyday
My wings are starting to fade away
I only see them in my dreams
I only feel their spirit
Longing just to feel it
I don't think I can stay here much longer
These feelings are growing stronger
I don't like being human
We do everything wrong
Too many sad songs
All the evil have the power
All the good trapped in evils little game
A game I steady play
Over and over again
Everyday a feather falls from my wings
One less uplifting song I will sing
I watch them wither
Once they disappear
The reason I love
Will no longer be here
Let Gabriel bring
The cure for my broken wings

Eat Your Cancer

I'm praying to bring down an angel
I need a feather
To get past this bad weather
Trying to trap a baby's breathe
The spirit of their first step
Fall in an earthquake
Mother earth is what I will take
I will drain my body of every ounce of blood
I can't live without your love
I will take you to every ocean
Inside steady hoping
I will travel to every sea
Just to help you believe
I will find every river's end
Do anything for my friend
Inside a tornado ill go
Bring back fear from this soul
Travel inside a hurricane
Bring back what makes me insane
Find a person close to death
To bring Gabriel back to you
Maybe he can tell me what to do
Climb to the mountain top
Praying I can make time stop
Travel through hell
On this quest I cannot fail
I will carry you in my arms to heaven's door
There on my knees on the floor
Somebody, someone tell me what to do
I just can't lose you
Sitting at your grave
In tears because I couldn't save
I hope you found someone to love

I often stare above
Every day I miss you more and more
sorry I couldn't find a way
To eat your cancer

\

The Forever Rose

A rose of thorns
Falling like a storm
The thorns full of blood
Dropping to meet the love
The undying rose
Just still and crying
Memories of the past
For the rose will forever last
The respect no regrets
Time stands still
For this moment of death
The rose the last one left
A goodbye and hello speak
For the rose tears start to leak
Think but the rose cannot speak
All the secrets
This flower will forever keep it
As it lays
On the ground it prays
Knowing it won't be see another day
The unconditional love inside the bud
Time on each petiole
For the final goodbye
And the last hello
It can never bloom again
To begin or end
The rose an eternal friend
The feeling that death has brought
For the last song that was sung
Only the lord knows
What will happen to the forever rose

Life

To live for this day
To live for this night
Thus a fight
A fight, to live your life
Is life just a dream
A nightmare it sometimes seem
Is life a gift
Or just something full of it
Should you quit and die
Or stay and try
Living is hard
Things can catch you off guard
It can be rough,
But on your life never give up
Live for your life
Live for this night
Live for this day
You only get one chance at life

Life Lessons

Everyday there is a lesson to learn
To learn you must figure it out
Whether your lesson is to learn
Or learn is your lesson
The best way to learn your lesson
Keep an open mind
Keep your eyes open
That little thing might be your lesson
So keep a watchful eye
It might catch you by surprise
Everyday is a lesson to learn
It is a test to strengthen
To keep you sharp
So remember your lesson
It might include life or death

Open Eyes

Two open windows see
The decimation of me
The eyes laugh
Waiting to penultimate destroy
The next to last
The last of my soul
To control cadaver
Leave me dead
In a loud bloody red
The eyes that are always watching
Who eyes
What eyes
Evil eyes that tells lies
Those evil eyes
Forever watching

Fallen Angel

An angel looks out
He wanted to be free in his eyes I see
He steps up to the almighty
My first angel
What is the problem?
Just curious you see
Just what is that over there that looks at me?
A human
But what is the need?
I need to spread my love
But why there is already enough above?
This is different they can never die
What do you mean?
What about the heart and the eye?
No for them I gave a soul
To live life after death
Can I get one of those?
There is no need you will forever be with me
The jealousy began to take hold
He must figure out how to take the soul
The plots the schemes
Filled the heavens with murderous things
Does the almighty
This can't be
Is there no more love for me?
You see in his eyes came the flame
To cause all humans
Nothing but pain
For the love lost from God
That can never be regain
The jealousy spreads
For all humans must be dead
But why must we defy the person who gave my eyes?
Fuck it the angel said

The words turned everyone head
A word to curse if heard it hurts
So are you with me?
Let's make God and all the humans' history
But he created you and me
Destroy God this can't be
Can't you see he doesn't love you or me?
No more words let conquer and destroy
No need to tell the rest
Some angels fell to the death
But still there is that one left
Eternal tangles
We will witness again
The tangle
A new chapter of the fallen angel

Untitled

Am I a fallen angel?
Fell to the earth and found hurt
Do I look up to the sky and ask why
Father I should have stayed home
I wanted love
So I came down from above
Was I wrong?
Was I right?
Here I hardly see any light
I pray, close my eyes
Hoping to see the place I left
I was dumb
I was 40 miles from the sun
I been here too many years
Gravity claiming all my tears
I feel contagious
I'm full of scar tissue
God, thy father I miss you
Purple stain porcelain
My only friend
Everything hurts so badly
Just sitting here trying to get the time to pass
Just too much on the mind
Is this my own prison?
This world is unforgiving
I'm torn
What is this life for?
What is my life for?
Can't seem to find a reason any more
I am a mind changer
To evil I have never been a stranger
I am war machine
I am a prize fighter
I need some light

Pass me a lighter
I'm somewhere between life and death
Fantasy and life
Reality and dreams
Nothing is what it seems
I'm trapped in the black rain
Suck in a black daze
This is my maze
There is a crack somewhere
That is how it got in
I can't seem to close
Hard to save my soul
I know it won't be easy
Everyone does not believe me
After I left heaven
I found myself in hell
Father told me it would be hard
Just keep your faith in me,
But I didn't know
All this temptation
Eternal damnation is what I am facing
All these things I want
Nothing, but lust
At least I have no greed,
But that makes it hard to eat
At least I have no hate
Things I let them get away
Look at me I am a sinner
Wash my flesh,
But still a sinner till my death
Clean my inside,
But still I find pride
I cross my heart and hope to die
Like the rose we clip
Just for a sniff
All my fears have come to life

All my fears have come to light
Everything I cured
Now I'm sick and bound
Some memories lost and found
I try to find comfort in these words
Not a single voice heard
I'm blind
Someone tell me the day and time
Like chapters in the bible
Many more are untitled

Schizophrenic

I hear voices in my head
I believe it's the call of the dead
Sounds of demon trying to break me
Give in to all my sins
Does anyone ever hear angels?
It has to be some type of connection
How come on one ever hears good voices
Beautiful sounds
Everyone thinks we are crazy
It's hard to silence the sounds
So hard to quiet the voices
Most of us left with three choices
Blow out your brains before you go insane
Take some meds
To get them out of your head
But the meds clouds your head
Feeling like the walking dead
Last you can fight
This step calls for long nights
Cause of long days
Keeps us lonely in my stay
Sometimes the voiced are so hard
All you can do is pray to God
Can get depressed easy
Makes you want to give up
There is only so much
That a person can take
Enough is enough
Sometimes we just give up
I wonder if everyone hears voices
But just too afraid to speak
A secret they will always keep
Sometimes I just want to scream
Shut up I had enough

Step outside my mind
Show yourself face me man to man
So you can feel the power of my hand
The strength of this man
But they never do
They never come out
Life sometimes hard to handle it
When you're schizophrenic

Forever Night

The sun falls
An never rise again
A beginning or an ending
Depends
To never see the sunlight
To see new things in the night
To be seen in a new way
All darkness, no light
To creep to crawl
Every time night falls
To live life as a shadow
Let day and night battle
No drop of light
To be cursed by the light
It overwhelms
Like the feeling of hell
To be cast out
You chose a path with one route
The wrong choice without a doubt
Eternally seeing
All your old memories leaving
no longer whole
The other half empty and hollow
When there is no light
There cannot be a tomorrow
Total darkness
Never a sight of relief
Now witness your defeat
Never a track of true sunlight
Trapped in the forever night

Forsaken

A disability
A lack of power
Can never stand tall like a tower
Disable
Life will always be unfit
Forever trapped in it
A disadvantage
Life has left me stranded
Disaffection
Everyone unfriendly to me
Always seems to disagree
No one ever wants to listen to me
Disallow
Never allow me to be free
Always disappoint
Never can seem to please
Disapproval
Almost everything I do
Disarm
So I can never do any harm
Disarrange
Putting all my thoughts out of order
Disassemble
Always trying to take me apart
A disaster
My life has seen nothing, but loss
Disavow
Deny all knowledge of how life used to be
Disband
Break up all I had
Disbar
Always taking things away from me
A disbelieve
No one ever believes in me

A discard
I'm useless for they throw me far
A disclaim
Refuse to recognize me as a person
Discomfit
Defeated completely no happiness for me
A discomfort
Seeming that I don't belong here
Discompose
Just confused and disturbed
Disconnected
Breaking all my connections in my life
So many things in my life they have taken
I know now that I'm forsaken

Follow the Wind

I lick my finger
Place it in the air
Follow the direction it blow
I have no home
Where I go I walk alone
Some say I'm a lost soul
But in the wind I found a home
I'm full of faith
God will guide my way
To a destine place
He alone controls my fate
The wind my only friend
Together till the end
Time waits for no man
But the wind waits for me
Together we roam free
I always win
When I follow the wind

Eternal Lovers (the story)

Two lovers missed
Life left them in a twist
These lovers lost
Will once again come to cross
It is their destiny
Life always seems to mess with thee
A curse that can never be broke
These two not lovers is a joke
Years and years
Yet they are still here
Be apart is something they never fear
By each other's side day and night
Even when separated by life
Always seeming to come back to each other
Like there is no other lover
Never can stay away long
Without each other
Their hearts can't go on
I guess this is their prophecy
In their eyes
Each other is all you see
How could this be?
Apart, but yet they still see
This must be magic
Without each other just tragic
The love for each other they can never past it
I guess they was chosen from birth
Any other love they will just be a curse
For them it just hurts
This connection that they have
Will never ever pass
Never together is a question they never ask
A choice I think they will never choose,
But together at the end of the road

I guess their story will forever be told
Seeming their love can never grow old
As young as the time
They first laid eyes
A first hello and never a last goodbye
This love can never die or fall
It will always stand tall
Forever like a journal
Lovers that are eternal

Lost Loves

For all my lovers missed
This is something I never will forget
For all the time we shared
Everlasting love beyond compare
For all the memories
I close my eyes and see
All the time spent by my side
Sometimes I want to cry
All in the past
In my mind will forever last
For the laugher
The ears we used to hear
The moments you lost fear
All the fun we had
Time went by fast
To all those that left
Be with me till my death
Like the rose I first touched
I gripped the thorns made my blood rush
This feeling that was giving
Makes me happy I'm living
If I could I would
Make you share my blood
Just for your love
I will spend myself above
This feeling can never be tossed
For all my lovers lost

Make this Poem Cry

I can't see a tear falling down my eye
So let me tell you how I feel inside
I shall miss you
Till my fire goes out
I long to kiss you
Soft lips can still feel the tips
A tingle in my hand
From the hips I used to grip
I'm haunted by your voice
This was not my choice
The side of your bed in graved with your curves
Oh how much I miss her
My rose full of thorns
Left more than my skin torn
I feel your breath on my neck
Hearing the sounds of your footsteps
The long walks through the park
The flowers no longer spark
The flowers no longer bloom
The blossoms never cherry
your smell left on my pillow
Laughter always heard
You always knew the word
I realize how much I miss you
As I pass by the tissue
I close my eyes
And make this poem cry

Murder in Mind

A day of blood and tears
Someone died without me
The trauma stops my heart beat
I felt pain
Water fell from the eye
The heart I thought I never had broke
Revenge, revenge
It's written in my heart
Till death did us part
The picture shows in the eye
But still he lives
In my blood, my heart, my mind, my soul
Can't let this one go
My tears can't even stop crying
Rest in peace
My fallen soldier see you at the crossroads
My mind snaps in total darkness or light
My schizophrenia
Voices tell me somebody has to die
Him or me
This disease this suffering
Psychopath no euthanasia
All pain
Running out of time
With murder in my mind

Timberwolves

In the woods at night
These figures
Creep and crawl
Shadows with glowing eyes
Hunters on the hunt
They purse till finally they get you
A chase
Loving the fear on your face
Once they start to track
There is no turning back
They search
Till their bones hurt
They track you down
In the woods their all around
Your never lost
Here always found
These dark stalkers
Night time day dreaming blood stalkers
Once in a while day stalkers
Seek
Just for flesh meat
Using every trail
So they can never fail
Forever on the prowl
When the suns goes down

Today's Story

Today's story
It's a wild profile
One dark day the wind blows
Sounds of evil spirits filled the air
Howling and woos
Music of a scary movie
Yellow and red a fiery sight filled the trees
The fire began to fall
It hit the ground
They dance all the way till they reached
It was a wonderful sight to see
The sky was pure yellow and red
Then the music stopped
A sound of thunder shock the ear drums
The sound of pain hurts the heart
The eyes poured tears
The sight was a sight for two soar eyes
Someone had died
That tree was a part of me

Silent Gun

What was that?
It cuts through the air with despair
Whatever it touches
Hits or make the blood rush
Come out without a doubt
Not a sound to worn
Not a sound to comfort the ear
Watch your back
You never know when it will pass
It last for a split second
No time is to waste
It never hesitates
It always catches haste
Speeds up pace
The more space
The more it will travel through this place
Never caring who or what it hits
Some things it hits
Some it will miss
If you see this you better be quick
Or meet up with it in an instant
Be warned
The speeds of a lightning storm
It seems like it is having fun
The sounds of a silent gun

Meaning of Life

The reason of living
The reason of my life
Why I wake up in the morning
What is the reason for me breathing?
Why should I care?
If I am here or there
Why do I dream?
Since everything ain't always what it seems
Why do I try to love?
Knowing I may never find
Why do I keep up with the time?
Is it because it's on my side
Why do I keep up with the days?
When everything doesn't go my way
Why do I even look?
All seems to get took
Why do I love?
Knowing they will be sent above
Why do I even think?
It will be gone with a blink
Why do I try?
Always seeming to cry
Why should I feel?
When I don't know what's real
Why should I touch?
When things seem to hurt so much
Why should I do?
Seeming it's not really my choice to choose
Why should I walk?
When I can go somewhere and talk
Why should I talk?
When I can go somewhere and walk
Why should I believe?
There is nothing I seem to see

Why should I be me?
They are just going to see what they want to see
Why should I go down that path?
I don't know if I will last
All these reasons why
The reasons and the meanings
Is to be happy
No one can tell you if you will last
Be happy follow your own path

Lord Knows

The only person that cares
My pain he bares
The only person to seem to know when I'm hurting
A person always in my heart
Death can never do us part
Inside my every thought
By my side on this earth
Trying to tell me
That I'm not cursed
He can recognize
Me by the eye
Hold my head when I cry
Tell me I will be safe when I die
Always understand
My feelings in this lost land
Always telling me I can
The only person who appreciate me for me
Always coming to talk to me in my dreams
Seems to remember everything I do
Now it is all for you
I admit sometimes I want to quit
That's the place he never lets me hit
I will always love him for this
He is there to sympathize
Every time a tear comes to my eye
He accept me for me
Something I thought I could never see
A sinner
But still he loves me
He seems to feel and sense
Every time I repent
He relates and shares his pain
Telling me there is a lot to gain
In his house I am never overlooked

Identifying the time it took
When I gather he gathers too
There's nothing else I rather do
Just to have one second with you
I behold and believe
His eyes are all I try to see
Hoping that he lives inside of me
Always trying to set me free
I don't know where I will go
Only the lord knows

End of the Road

A person runs,
Runs like they never ran before
Not a second to think
I never even seen him blink
His heart beats fast
Loud like thunder
Will he get tired I wonder
His blood races
His pulse lows
But still he never slows
His pain seem to grow
His soul starts to glow
As I watch
I feel his pain in my heart
So I start to follow
His feeling inside
Seems to be hollow
Empty for some reason I had to see
His eyes red
A look in his eyes like he's dead
But still he runs
What is the reason
I must know
What is making him go
He has this need not to breathe
Why does this interest me
Feeling as if I'm witnessing his Destiny
Till finally he stops
What would make him stop?
Then here he dropped
Why would he run so far to stop now?
Till finally I found
Because no one was around

All I Can't Leave Behind

It will come a time
That I will have to say goodbye
And take all I can't leave behind
I will take a few CD's
To listen too
When I write all my creeds
I will take my clothes
Back to the wind when it blows
Millions more miles to walk in my shoes
I will take risen power
My life, my love, my soul
One day find my way home
I will take a picture of the one that I love
Is it the one that doesn't want me?
And my child I adore
Every second I will miss them more and more
I will take my camcorder
To record the past time
Birds to share my lonely view
I will bring a few books
Mostly poetry and butterflies
To help me fly
I will take me
The many things I shall see
Once again I will vanish
A lost soul without a home
I will wonder on
From dusk till dawn
I will travel so far
My two feet no car
Many countries I will see
Guatemala the first and the last
At the end of my quest

An unmarked grave
Buried on the side of an volcano
My body will find his home
My grave marked with a single rose
Even though the love still grows
The home of a lost soul
Give away everything that is mines
Only taking
The one thing I couldn't leave behind

All I See

Tunnel is my vision
I view things in a narrow path
I see straight no left, no right
What I view
Is always right in my sight
I only see what I want to see
The snow could fall
When the rain comes down
Still never obstruct my view
What I see is true to me
Nothing can get me off my path
Walk it till my last
The end of this tunnel
Is all I see

On My Knees

Forgive me father
For I have sinned against thee
There's no comfort within me
I danced with the devil
I stayed at his right hand
I no longer want to be
Apart of his land
I'm tired of all the lies
And watching the people I love die
This world can go to hell
But I don't want to go with it
I watch people burn
But never ever learn
All the fire
Will eventually make me expire
I did so many wrongs
I can count the rights
Only eleven so far from heaven
I am one step from hell
So many times
I almost tripped and fell
My life one big caution sign
Walking on the thin red line
I heard when you go from hell to heaven
Demons will follow
Trying to cloud your tomorrows
Whispering in your ears
All the things you fear
But I'm ok with that
I will do anything
I just want my life back
Help me believe
I am on my knees

Bloody Secrets

Inside us all lies bones
A story that will never tell
A bone, alive and breathing
Watching
Only a few have seen it
To never speak those words
Death to whomever speaks the words
A tail that should never be told
All the answers lies at the end of the road
A secret, so secret
Those who know should keep it
Bloody as a bed of roses
For those who choose to lose
Beware some never care
Some will tell the tail
The one who really knows
Heaven and hell
Locked away chained
For the day their past meets again
The key thrown away
Lost can never be found
A secret you dread
I can make you lose your head
No lies
Just not letting anyone inside
A nightmare, no dream
It seems that you will always keep it
That bloody secret

Another Death

Another day
Another death
Everyday someone dies
It happens so much
On one ever cries
Sometimes no one cares
Death should have no fears
We are all better off that way
No more fear
No more tears
No more pain and sorrow
Not having to worry about tomorrow
No more grief
No more watching
Family and friends decease
Everyday someone has to die
It might be you
Another night
Another death

Cause of Death

The bane was clear
Quail back in fear
It was a setup
His lover lead him to the tryst
That was secret so he thought
Caught by surprise
Death rose into his eye
He died
His heart broke apart
His heart fell
When she said they have to part
Then she left
He had to deal
With his cause of death

Circle of Pain

An angle
That is full of tangles
Full of ups and downs
What is the reason of this stuff
I already had so much
Enough is enough
This that loves to rush
Like a blood lust
360 degrees
Till one day takes a toll on me
It starts at a point moves
Turns and reach the point of return
This point
I wish will never return
Go away
Don't come back another day
A circle that turns
Make my eyes burn
Hate for those who create
They say no pain, no gain
What will I gain
In this circle of pain

Death Only the Beginning

Death
Not the ending
But a beginning
A new life
A life to replace your old
Now a new story is told
A launching for a new dawn
Forever this life will go on
Restores your mind
Memories you left behind
A fresh new start
The new and the old must be a part
A new birth
Finally you leave this earth
This intro
An opening in your life
Such a wonderful new light
A creation
That many people are waiting
No longer an ending
Death truly a new beginning

Death

Please take me another day
I not ready to go
I love my life
I want my soul
Everything I have is yours
Stop knocking at my door
Whatever you want I don't have
I wish you just came to pass
I'm not ready
Look my heart still beats steady
Look I still have life left
Listen to my protest
You can't make me go
It's my body, it's my soul
No forget what I just said
I take it all back
Please just let me breathe
I'm not ready to leave
I know there's nothing I can do
Just wish I could convince you
I'm not ready to take this step
Don't take me O death

My Death

It feels like my time
Just too weak to hind
Plus anyway they will find
I'm losing my sight
Someone say
Is it day or night
I'm getting old
Can feel myself
Starting to get cold
My new life I will behold
I wish it would wait a year or two
Still some things I want to do
A lot of regrets
I'm still regretting
At least I could say
I been there done that
Travel through hell and back
I lost every single fear
For so long I lived here
It's getting kind of hard to breathe
Can feel every ounce of air leave
My bones are brittle
My skin is old
I hear a voice
It's time to come home
My DNA no longer resists
This life
We both had enough of it
My DNA no longer wants to make up
I know if I go to sleep
I will not wake up
I can feel deaths rusty hand
Ready to take me to his land
Gabriel in bones comes to take me home

It's time for my last rest
Death

O Death

A plane fall and ended it all
I watched another crash
The building and the people didn't last
I watched a newborn baby die
Still brings tears to my eye
I watched someone get shot
In my arms they bled from the head
I watched another get stabbed
Dying talking about all the fun they had
I watched a child get hit by a car
His mother wasn't too far
I watched a girl get raped
Shouldn't have went out on that date
I watched a serial killer do his job
He won't be seeing God
I watched terrorist tare a hole in the world
Sleep now sweet little girl
They say it's in the name of God
That's odd I never heard that when he talk
These are the moments I live for
The hatchet to take the souls to hell
I take them there
It's where they will dwell
I never rest
They call me O death

Gabriel

It's my name
But now I found fame
I have many different names
But all mean the same
I'm in many places at once
I'm very upfront and blunt
I always get what I want
I'm the bringer and the taker
Never a forsaker
I'm not by any means racists
All that matter to me is the faces
I been here seen the first human being
My job I feel for some is best
Some are better off in death
My hatchet and my rusty hand
In some I take pleasure
Taking to no man's land
I'll come in bones
To take them to their new home
I have no remorse
I'm the world's eternal curse
I take away or bring all hurt
All the babies and children
I hold them close
They never got live
To all the evil
I long to touch
Taking their breath away is a must
To all the good ones I love to set free
Finally they get to see what I see
I am not the judge
But still feel hate and love
I will see every single face
I will touch ever single soul

Whether young or old
I leave them all cold
I am the soul taker not the keeper
They all call me the reaper

Break Bread

To the ones I love
I offer you blessings from above
This action is a act of love
It's a blessing to sit at this table
It is a honor to be here with you
For you to be here with me
Today we dine
Pass the bottle of wine
Toast to our living Ghost
Give thanks to our host
No enemy can sit in this chair
Only the ones we care
The meaning of this feast is deep
When I pass this glass
Time to let go of the past
When I hand you a plate
Let go of all your hate
Once you pull up that chair
Time to let down your hair
The cause of this brings nothing but love
Don't reach out you hand
If you truly don't understand
I can offer you nothing better from this man
Pour oil on your head
Time to break

Psalms

I believe in my creed
With every drop of blood
With every ounce of love
Oh God life is hard
It's hard being me
But not hard to believe
I live with the eye of the spirit
I live with the heart of the son
I live with the love of the everlasting
I'm a sinner ain't no doubt about it
Every day I breathe I wake up
A sinner
But always I processed to be a winner
I look to the sky say a few words
Crash my love on the curve
I try to live my life to the fullest
After all it's a gift
The best present ever giving
A blessing to just be living
So many friends and family no longer here
But in my dreams and prayers your still there
To God I'll always sing my songs
My psalms

Never Had

Sometimes I sit back and often wonder
Would my life had been different
If life was never given
If I had someone to hold and touch
A person to open up their arms and hug me
Just a person to always tell that they love me
A mother to share my pain
A brother to share my blood
It seems all is far from love
My life in two words
Messed up
Everyday looking for death
Seems I will be the last one left
All the demons in my mind screaming
All the voices I hear
I had it up to here
All the darkness that surrounds
Knowing it will bring me down
All nightmares no dreams
I look forward to these things
All the hurt and pain
Knowing I can never be the same
A person
Without a heart
Tell death did us part
In the shadow of death
A life between life and death
Always a feeling of loneliness
Keeps me so depressed
Have no reason to live
But all the reasons to die
My eyes so dark
Look to long an my life story will start
A heart that has never been whole

Just an empty hole
Seeming to get bigger day by day
So I often try to keep people away
My feeling not taking, but giving
I may never get a chance
Because my life is not worth living
A brain that is insane
So when I speak I scream
No pleasure, all pain
Please God don't let me live this life again
Seems like I am troublesome
Always forgetting the times I had fun
Always feeling never needed
All memories come on so fast
Not good, all bad
A soul that is just sad
Happiness something I never had

Right My Wrongs

Don't think this poem
Can go on that long
I been wrong
I did wrong
There is a difference
Of being wrong and doing wrong
I'm guilty of doing both
But never gave up hope
Sometimes it's hard to cope
Like I'm addicted to dope
Hey if it wasn't for
The things I didn't do right
I probably have nothing to write
I probably wouldn't feel this pain
I hope someone, somewhere has something to gain from
my pain
I wish I could find
The all the ones I did wrong
Will I have time to tell them all?
I was wrong

A Reason

There is a reason
Things go bump in the night
The things you fear without the light
There you are in total fright
Beware,
Things appear here and there
There are no warnings
Don't blink or start to think
They appear
They can smell your fear
Never close your eyes
Closer and closer by your side
There they enter your mind
You can run, but not hide
In all darkness they can find
Night time they say is all mines
This is their time
Always concealed,
But never hidden
Your phobia they can feel
Your anxiety
Knowing they are right beside me
The horror you dread
Knowing they are standing over your head
The terror in your brain
Will slowing drive you insane
There under your bed
They are messing with your head
This figure so shadowy and murky
Concerned that someone cursed me
Just the beating of your hear
There is a reason to be scared of the dark

Money Talks

In God we trust
The money is God
The money is all we trust
A piece of paper
A tree runs the world
It runs my life
It runs your life
It makes you kill
It makes you steal
It's pure evil and it talks
Don't let anything stand in your way
Of you and me
Greed enters the soul
Green is all my eyes seen
Money talks the talk
I'm going to walk with the talk

An Initiation

A life taken is what you're facing
To be a part
A part you must have heart
Have the quality of lion
Let no one stand in your way
Be lupine wolf like with insight
To nihilism the law
To die for the cause
To be down whatever
Whatever, whenever
Are you ready?
Are you ready?
Do except this test
An initiation is what you are facing

The Last Words

My last words
What would I say?
Good or bad still my last
Will it be a memory?
For someone other than me
Will it be joke?
Some words I never spoke
Will it be a war cry?
Or something I been waiting to say when I die
Will anyone be around?
When my last words
Start to come down
Will it be?
To tell my love ones
This is something I have to see
My last words
Something to think about
If I can
A tear to tell everyone I care
After all a tear speaks for itself
I just hope someone is around to hear
My last words

Beauty

Sight or sound
This is all around
Surrounds all eyes
Sometimes lies inside
Sometimes on the outside
A flower, a rose
This tell forever told
A gift for eyes
If you see it enough you can gladly die
A wonderful sight to see
Sometimes a wonderful thing to feel
Always asking is this real
Is this heaven sent
The way my eyes seem to repent
A wonder of how this came to be
A life long journey for you and me
The things you see every day
Will now give off the way
A touch of something soft
Can sometimes leave you lost
A blessing for the eyes to have sight
At the break of day or the dawn of night
This picture, mysterious figure
Lights up the eyes
Knowing the best way to kept it
Just let in fly
This lifelong companion
Always thankful I had a chance to have it
This uncontrollable feeling
My eyes and ears are doing the dealing
A lifetime of tears
Happiness throughout the years
Amazing the only word my eyes use to describe
A dream in eyes I see

Music to my ears
The sound of that voice
Can make you lose your fears
A touch that I want so much
The soft embrace
Just the smile on the face
Never can tell how your eyes will see
When it come face to face with beauty

Sweet Desire

It hurts so bad
It's something I have to have
I must touch
I must hold
When it comes, never let it go
Without this by my side
I feel I will die
Nothing can stop me
Or stand in my way
There is no escape
This craving that I have
Can never ever pass
I yearn
I long for this
I shall never quit
This extreme need
I love yes indeed
I'm obsessed
I will settle for nothing less
This ache that I feel
Seems to heal
This want that I have
Rushes through so fast
This tie that binds
I have to make this mine
This sensation
Causes no hesitation
Grant me mercy I beg
Let me have this emotion
Like the sand has the ocean
This ambition
This appetite
This urge
This feeling that I'm cursed

Continues to keep me in the mood
I don't know what to do
Inside full of fire
Oh please sweet desire

Turning Stairway

In the dark
I begin to walk
The walk was long
How long will this go on?
I could not even see
My hand right in front of my face
What is this place?
All of a sudden
I see a light
The light separate from the night
Like true day and night
I felt a presence
I had a chill
A person walked by
Right into the light
I stop it was at the crossroads
I looked up
An endless turning stairway
With a tower of souls

I began to glow
Oh my, I am a soul
My heart stopped
Or at least what was my heart
I felt a calmness enter this soul
As if I knew which way to go
I seen beauty before,
But this was so much more
As I stared in the air
There was no other care
I could not see the top of the stairway
So many things I wanted to say,
But I didn't speak a word
Things still seem to be heard

The stairway was very high
Infused into the sky
For some reason I started to cry
Everybody else moving
I'm in a stand still could this be real

I started to walk
Side by side
Today together we have died
So it is true
Meet you at the other side
I had many dreams
To heaven I walked up steps,
But they never looked like this
The steps still, floating in the air
Up and down the structure
Was a golden pole
The reflection for the souls
Every step I took
A memory came over me
How, so many things I have forgot
How many things I will miss
Oh, how many I want to forget
I spiraled around
Steady looking down
There was no more ground
I reached the end of the stairway
All my tears turned to diamonds
My soul no longer glowed
Finally I am truly home
Nice I never had a home
The things I seen I can't describe
I traveled so far
In my hand I held a star
So this is where I belong
Now waiting for you to come

To the stairway to heaven

Final Fantasy

A last wish
A last dream
Your final thoughts
A ending to your story
Finally to finish
To think no more on it
A happy ending
A happy ending
Like the time of your beginning
If this is all I do
I hope this come true
This closing part of my life
Just to set things right
This vision in my mind
I hope I find the time
To make this last thing mine
Imagine this
I will be happy
If this in my life is all I get
This mirage
Makes my life less hard
This invention
In which I'm always wishing
That it will come true
The last thing I want to do
A conclusion to my question
Let me teach this lesson
If this is my last move
Then this is what I choose
This dream from me
Could only be
My final fantasy

Do What You Want

This life
Your life
My life
Once you truly know wrong and right
Tell them to stay out
It's mine
Only I can stand the test of time
All the choices up to you
Do what you want to do
Life is full of risks
It's up to you to get a grip
No one can tell you
What makes you happy but you
So go find what makes you, you
Your heart is free so follow
No one can say if you will live tomorrow
Live for your life
So what if it's wrong or right
Your happiness means more than you know
So go
Make time to heal your soul
Put your life in your own control
There your story will unfold
Your life is too great
Never let it go
Fly go be free
No one can tell you what to see
Or who or what is your destiny
The future is all up to you
The past there is nothing you can do
Stand proud
Scream this is my life
And be very blunt
This is my life

And I will do what I want

Understanding God

This is hard
Maybe the hardest poem I will ever write
But here we go
I am reaching into my soul
How could he let this happen?
Who am I to run your life?
But you are God
Yes but still your will is free
It doesn't come from me
But still you should come to me
Why don't you show your face?
On this world I want no trace
But you, your four fathers lied
They forsake so myself I took
Just read the book
Yes and about that
Everything in there isn't true
But you still know what to do
Why do we die?
Two reasons
This is not your real life
Not this one only the next
This one is just a step
So always watch your step
Yes but don't you love us
Yes I really do
Still cannot control the things you do
Help us find our way
First you must help yourself
I am the way
But I will not show you the way
Most people don't believe
And if you don't believe
I cannot help you breathe

I watch people come and leave
Centuries of man
All I held in my hand
What are your views on war?
Depends on what you're fighting for
Freedom I always understand
But never to take a land
Or to just kill a fellow man
You can't see the way my eyes bleed
Whenever you feel the need
To make another soul bleed
Loving you is hard true indeed
So why did you let your son die
That wasn't my choice
He chose that on his own
He wondered why you do the things you do
He found out the hard way
Trying to resist sin everyday
He learned that the flesh
Was imperfect to the bone
His life and death
The greatest gift that was found
Gave you humans away back home
It isn't very hard
To understand God

Visions

Foresight
In day or night
My view of life is different
Imagine something there
But you cannot see
My eyes see things only for me
A image pure relentless
A daydream I often do this
A prophecy in my eyes I see
In no time starts to haunt my mind
A revelation in my eyes I am facing
A concept that is there till my death
No one ever sees but me
Some must think I'm crazy
They try to keep away
So they won't see me snap today
Some come fast
Some come slow
But still in my mind all real
Dreams or nightmares
Had them so long I no longer fear
My vision so clear
Appear there and here
I stop, look, and listen
Always having visions

Share My World

Take my hand
Follow me to my land
Lose all your fears
Hoping you never shed a tear
Come see what I see
How beautiful you look
In my eyes to me
Come walk a mile in my shoes
I will leave
All the choices up to you
Journey through my mind
See how you are on my mind all the time
Come touch my soul
Maybe you can help all my troubles
Come share my memories
And see what makes up me
Come share my pain
So I won't have to
Look back on it again
Come share my blood
So you can forever feel the love
Come and touch my heart
Maybe you can keep it from falling a part
Come and see my tears
Maybe you can take away all my fears
Come listen to the voices inside my mind
Make them shut up
So everything can be fine
Come and become one with me
So I can be whole
And have two pair of eyes to see
Just come and be with me
Just please
Share my world with me

Wild December

The hunter's moon
The winter's moon
Witness doom
For those who feel it
It's hunted or hunter
For those with a wild spirit
Only you can feel it
For those
You stand out in the cold
Like a wolf
You have a cold stare
But beware hunters are hunted too
But you know
It's just the law
Survival of the fittest
The code for hunters to follow
So they can taste tomorrow
Choose your own path
Hunters on the prowl
This happens every winter
World be prepared for a wild December

Wild Times

Life is a jungle
Animals surviving by instinct
Humans animals are we not
Human instinct
To cheat
To steal
To lie
To kill
To love
To hate
To be both good and evil
To create and destroy
The jungle is the city
Crime
Murder
Hopelessness
Stealing
Lying
Hating
Lord knows we all love to hate
Everything crazy
In these wild times

Ashes and Dust

I hear we are all dust in the wind
But it is much more my friend
All the trees once a seed
Places where people bleed
Some believed in a creed
Graveyards of the lost
Some graves are found
Known places where their body lays down
Nothing last but the earth and the stars
Their dreams reached so far
Every step you take
Has once been taken
Paths lost and forsaken
The families of the living
Life and love and still given
They cleanse the air
They wash away the sand
They freeze the land
Blowing the wind for new man
In this land I trust
We are much more
Than ashes and dust

Excuses

We all have excuses
Which are truly useless
The things we did
In which we cannot live
Are reasons for being dumb
Another excuse for being young
Our reasons have no real reasons
We can't deal with
Truly hard to live with
We sometimes tend to lose our way
When the truth is all in you
Your excuse hidden deep away
A guilty feeling
The only time you pray
If you just nipped it in the butt
Then you wouldn't have ran out of luck
We all need to grow up
We tend to lose this
Cover our acts with excuses

Born From Blood

This country is born from blood
That can never wash away
Goes back to the first day
We killed Native Americans
For no reason
The first day
Our so called beloved country
First started the bleeding
We bathe the land in blood
Showing not a single drop of love
They enslaved my people
Whipped and burned us to the ground
Look your country is paying now
Our politicians use to duel
Get played like a fool
Endless numbers of death
Just to be the best
Even this great country
They could care less
There can never be love
When you are born from blood

For Which it Stands

I love what it stands for
But I hate what it is
This country not a great place to live
Justice and freedom for all men
But no love for my kin
Black and Latin
Hurting, weathered calloused to the bone
This has never been our home
Everything I got it came the hard way
Nothing for free or easy
But want me to give to them everyday
My middle finger I keep it raised
Peace without a piece
Ain't no way
I see the flag raised
Only the military I gave praise
They helped us in so many ways
I am a believer in the country's spirit
Not the body
True essence lies within the soul
Until that is found
Once again not a home
Stuck digging up graveyards alone
I'm searching for George Washington
Martin Luther king
Searching for that dream
No more nightmares
I want it to be seen
Checking unmarked graves
All of the slaves
Look through their eyes
And find where true hope lies
I see God on money
But not in the country

My God loves
Here all I see is hate
I love the fact that I am mixed
Black, white, Native American and Spanish
We all need this
We all should mix
Then how could you hate a race
Find the same on every face
I am a madman with a diary
So I write what's inside of me
I am loved, hated and feared
God will always live here
I care so much I lose hair
Maybe my kids will change the world
When all the old evil go to hell
Maybe my true country can prevail
I shall live through my kids
A generation, an empire of freedom fighters
Is what you are facing
An to the republic
For which it stands
Until the nation is under God
Never stopping liberty
And justice for all

Soldier

In America we may not always agree
But in you I believe
Pray for a safe return
When you leave
The voice of America that breathe
Once again in you I believe
Fight the good fight
I am praying for your life
You didn't start the war
Your the cause that I will fight for
Never wonder if we miss you when you're gone
If we love you when you're gone
The real Americas for you sing songs
Our freedom fighters
We don't need no light you are the lighter
I pray for your safe return
I want your body with your soul to knock on the door
So I will see no ribbons at the door
One day the world may change
So your families you won't be astray
Keep your head up high
Keep your shoulders square
Stick your chest out
In you I never doubt
I never show my pride
Till a veteran walks by my side
So many of you didn't and won't come home
But you are not alone
This soil always your home
Family and friends there to hold you
A salute to all the past, present, and future soldiers

9/11

I watched an evil act
A day we can never get back
They tried to instill fear
But you lost, no fear lives here
You lost, only love lives here
I plant my flag let it blow in the wind
Because we didn't let you win
Everyday a new flag is raised
In honor of that tragic day
So much anguish you caused
At all the life that was lost
You didn't succeed
Nothing stronger than a heart that bleeds
In the strength of the families that lost we believe
Watching their strength with every breath they breathe
We lost mothers, fathers, sons, and daughters
But once again I tell you, you lost
United we stand
Together we shall fall
You tried to divide
But only strength you have provide
See the power in the eye
Feel the prosperity in every tear we cry
This day will never be lost
This day will never be forgotten
Can't erase the pages
History may repeat
But you will never win
That history is destine to repeat
I hope I find you all in heaven
The victims of 9/11

Revolutionary

I plant my flag
The flag and the wind will become one
I don't need to wave it in the air
It now belongs to the wind
Still there
Even after I win
I won at the start
Planted my flag with my heart
The courage it took
My flag placed
Made the ground shook
Today I am history
Until the stars go dim
The stars shall never go dim
Now I am one of the stars
The old stars now shine for me
Today I set my soul free
At that single moment I started to believe
The first time I truly breathe
The life in my lungs will never leave
I shall face destiny
Stare death right in the eye
No tear I shall cry
Gabriel is now on my side
Time is now on my side
This equivalent exchange
My life to stand for what is right
I am now held in the hand
I can see in total darkness
I bring darkness to light
From now on I shall fight
The kings will gather to my grave
A peaceful ground for the slaves
I shall never be a remnant

I am a pillar
A plot for war
No longer a king of sorrow
I am the king of tomorrow

Youth is Wasted on the Young

All we want to do is have fun
Steady we drink and never think
we never want to hear the truth
Even though it will set us free
We say let me be me
We touch the fire knowing it's hot
We tend to get burned a lot
We always think someone is trying to control us
When it's the truth they tell us
We never see things
Right in front of our faces
We see nothing but empty spaces
We never see harm until we're harmed
We will ignore the alarm
Our spider sense will tingle
in danger we still mingle
We are always in the wrong place
At the wrong time
Always thinking this life is mine
We're selfish to the point
that nothing matters but us
A lot of us die young
Killing the families only son
It's our fault because we never think
Death is just a blink
We have love ones behind
in their grief they go blind
We think fun is drugs and alcohol
Setting ourselves up for a fall
That sometimes we can't pick ourselves up from
So many of my family and friends
died by the gun
My cousin is jail
For killing someone because he choose to drink and drive

Leaving his poor son
With pain in his eye
I can't imagine
how much he made that family cry
If only he could turn back the hands of time
Behind the wheel he change his mind
There is tons of other ways to have fun
Get a got job and buy everything you want
Start a family raise your kids
Teaching them the right ways to live
But no we like to live with regrets
eating a hole in our souls
Till there is nothing left
We never listen to our elders
the right things they tell us
We you start the right path when you're young
Even in old age you have fun
When you make too many mistakes when you're young
Life being older is never fun
So many regrets there in your death
in this life you only get one
Youth is wasted on the young

Who Would Ever Want to be King

All hail the king
All hail the king
The song the people sing
All bow before his feet
On their knees you find them
A king cannot commit sin
It was written in the bible
I will never believe that till my end
So many tyrants before me
Did not let the people free
I don't want to rule with an iron fist
But I don't want to lose my grip
There is no answer to this question
There is no answer to this secret
If so in death the past kings keep it
So much pressure
I truly hold this world on my shoulder
I hold this world in my palm
A week can't go by
Without hearing the alarm
This crown on my head is heavy
My own crown of thorns
I long for death on the battlefield
A sweet release
No more bowing at my feet
I long to fight
But they make me stay home
My dark room with a throne
So many wars lost
So many battles I win
I trust no one
Steady longing for a friend
New songs I wish they sing
Who would ever want to be king

When I Ruled the World

The sun rise
When I awake
The moon appears
When I tell it to
There is no mystery
I wrote all the words in history
No land was uncharted
To worlds lost I departed
Not a heart I didn't find space
The hero of all heroes
In my numbers
There was no zeros
The birds sang for me
The butterflies asked me
If they could be free
I never said I was sorry
I was never wrong
When I walked you heard my theme song
When I dreamed never a nightmare
These eyes never shed a tear
I destroyed all fear
I made fear, fear
Death please, he passed me
And bowed to his knees
Was it all a dream
Or was I once a king

Hero

Mine doesn't live in the form of a man but a woman
She held my heart in her hand
By my side
As a little boy who would never cry
She made me tough
Never helped me up
Always told me to get up
Always believed in me
Even in my lost soul times
I could not see
My rock
Who made me a rock
When together we create a spark
She brings light to a room
Brings love to my heart
Even the times I fell a part
There on the steps in the ghetto
Teaching me how to read
Beside a little boy
When no one else wanted me
She sacrificed everything to give me life
I was her world
She was the only world this little child had
She took me to her job
I know I made her life hard
But never did she up
Never did she leave my side
Wiping all my tears when I finally cried
Telling is ok to shed a tear
It can help you lose that fear
Release the anger from here
Just a blessing to have her here
Unconditional love felt through a tight hug
In my life no other my grandmother

No it's more, my mother
Hand across the lip
Because my tongue I like to spit
Wonder where I got that tongue
This gift to run my lip
The smartest, strongest, kind hearted person I ever known
The day she goes
Take a part of my heart
Take a part of my soul
Feel her touch with the wind has it blows
I will always love my hero

New Hero

You know my hero
A smile there goes my hero
She's nothing but special ordinary
The things learned burned in my soul
Now I follow my daughter where she goes
My pride and joy
Now she gives me life
Love her wrong or right
There to wipe all her tears
Help her to master her fears
Hand across her lip
I wonder where she gets it from
Loves to run that tongue
On the playground
Till the sun goes down
As a child run to me
Set my spirit free
Me and my baby girl can move some shoes
Walk miles in our shoes
Another rock creating another
When together you will feel the spark
I would have never known
Someone else could find my soul
Make a home in my heart
She found a way at the start
In my arms protect her from harm
Do this even if I'm wrong
In the morning for years
Get her ready for school
Caught in a game of fools
It was like waking the dead
Comb my baby's hair
Drop her off at school
There to pick her up

Her I could never have enough
Beside me with the TV
Rub her head till the sand man comes
To lay her down on the bed
Felt like putting out my sun
My little girl is no longer little
Full of hopes and dreams
Never stop talking about hair things
I sigh, smile and shake my head looking at the sky
I understand now
I thought my hero held my heart in her hand
But that's not true
Because my child holds my heart
She may not understand the things I do for her now
How much I sacrificed so much of my life
How much I love her
But maybe one day she will
Feeling my touch with the wind as it blows
Maybe I will be her hero